Cloud Database
Complete Self-Assessment Guide

The guidance in this Self-Assessment is based on best
practices and standards in business process architecture, design and
quality management. The guidance is also based on the professional
judgment of the individual collaborators listed in the Acknowledgments.

Table of Contents

About The Art of Service

The Art of Service, Business Process Architects since 2000, is dedicated to helping stakeholders achieve excellence.

Defining, designing, creating, and implementing a process to solve a stakeholders challenge or meet an objective is the most valuable role… In EVERY group, company, organization and department.

Unless you're talking a one-time, single-use project, there should be a process. Whether that process is managed and implemented by humans, AI, or a combination of the two, it needs to be designed by someone with a complex enough perspective to ask the right questions.

Someone capable of asking the right questions and step back and say, 'What are we really trying to accomplish here? And is there a different way to look at it?'

With The Art of Service's Standard Requirements Self-Assessments, we empower people who can do just that — whether their title is marketer, entrepreneur, manager, salesperson, consultant, Business Process Manager, executive assistant, IT Manager, CIO etc... —they are the people who rule the future. They are people who watch the process as it happens, and ask the right questions to make the process work better.

Contact us when you need any support with this Self-Assessment and any help with templates, blue-prints and examples of standard documents you might need:

http://theartofservice.com
service@theartofservice.com

Included Resources - how to access

Included with your purchase of the book is the Cloud Database

Self-Assessment Spreadsheet Dashboard which contains all questions and Self-Assessment areas and auto-generates insights, graphs, and project RACI planning - all with examples to get you started right away.

How? Simply send an email to
access@theartofservice.com
with this books' title in the subject to get the Cloud Database Self Assessment Tool right away.

You will receive the following contents with New and Updated specific criteria:

• The latest quick edition of the book in PDF

• The latest complete edition of the book in PDF, which criteria correspond to the criteria in...

• The Self-Assessment Excel Dashboard, and...

• Example pre-filled Self-Assessment Excel Dashboard to get familiar with results generation

• In-depth specific Checklists covering the topic

• Project management checklists and templates to assist with implementation

Purpose of this Self-Assessment

This Self-Assessment has been developed to improve understanding of the requirements and elements of Cloud Database, based on best practices and standards in business process architecture, design and quality management.

It is designed to allow for a rapid Self-Assessment to determine how closely existing management practices and procedures correspond to the elements of the Self-Assessment.

The criteria of requirements and elements of Cloud Database have been rephrased in the format of a Self-Assessment questionnaire, with a seven-criterion scoring system, as explained in this document.

In this format, even with limited background knowledge of Cloud Database, a manager can quickly review existing operations to determine how they measure up to the standards. This in turn can serve as the starting point of a 'gap analysis' to identify management tools or system elements that might usefully be implemented in the organization to help improve overall performance.

How to use the Self-Assessment

On the following pages are a series of questions to identify to what extent your Cloud Database initiative is complete in comparison to the requirements set in standards.

To facilitate answering the questions, there is a space in front of each question to enter a score on a scale of '1' to '5'.

1 Strongly Disagree

2 Disagree

3 Neutral

4 Agree

5 Strongly Agree

Read the question and rate it with the following in front of mind:

'In my belief, the answer to this question is clearly defined'.

There are two ways in which you can choose to interpret this statement;
1. how aware are you that the answer to the question is clearly defined
2. for more in-depth analysis you can choose to gather evidence and confirm the answer to the question. This obviously will take more time, most Self-Assessment users opt for the first way to interpret the question and dig deeper later on based on the outcome of the overall Self-Assessment.

A score of '1' would mean that the answer is not clear at all, where a '5' would mean the answer is crystal clear and defined. Leave emtpy when the question is not applicable or you don't want to answer it, you can skip it without affecting your score. Write your score in the space provided.

After you have responded to all the appropriate statements in each section, compute your average score for that section, using the formula provided, and round to the nearest tenth. Then transfer to the corresponding spoke in the Cloud Database Scorecard on the second next page of the Self-Assessment.

Your completed Cloud Database Scorecard will give you a clear presentation of which Cloud Database areas need attention.

Cloud Database
Scorecard Example

Example of how the finalized Scorecard can look like:

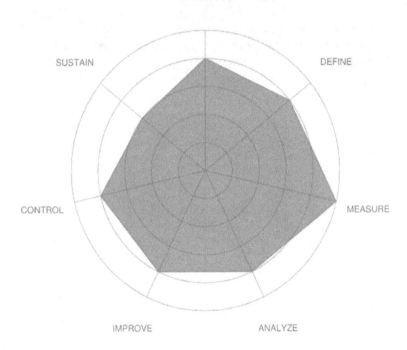

Cloud Database
Scorecard

Your Scores:

BEGINNING OF THE SELF-ASSESSMENT:

CRITERION #1: RECOGNIZE

INTENT: Be aware of the need for change. Recognize that there is an unfavorable variation, problem or symptom.

In my belief, the answer to this question is clearly defined:

5 Strongly Agree

4 Agree

3 Neutral

2 Disagree

1 Strongly Disagree

1. Which information does the Cloud Database business case need to include?
<--- Score

2. Does the problem have ethical dimensions?
<--- Score

3. How can auditing be a preventative security measure?

<--- Score

4. How do you recognize an objection?
<--- Score

5. Can management personnel recognize the monetary benefit of Cloud Database?
<--- Score

6. To what extent does each concerned units management team recognize Cloud Database as an effective investment?
<--- Score

7. What is the problem or issue?
<--- Score

8. Is it needed?
<--- Score

9. Who needs to know about Cloud Database?
<--- Score

10. What information do users need?
<--- Score

11. Who defines the rules in relation to any given issue?
<--- Score

12. Are there Cloud Database problems defined?
<--- Score

13. What are the clients issues and concerns?
<--- Score

14. To what extent would your organization benefit from being recognized as a award recipient?
<--- Score

15. Are employees recognized for desired behaviors?
<--- Score

16. Who needs what information?
<--- Score

17. Is the quality assurance team identified?
<--- Score

18. How are the Cloud Database's objectives aligned to the group's overall stakeholder strategy?
<--- Score

19. What Cloud Database problem should be solved?
<--- Score

20. How are you going to measure success?
<--- Score

21. Will it solve real problems?
<--- Score

22. Who are your key stakeholders who need to sign off?
<--- Score

23. Do you need different information or graphics?
<--- Score

24. What should be considered when identifying available resources, constraints, and deadlines?
<--- Score

25. What do employees need in the short term?
<--- Score

26. How do you recognize an Cloud Database objection?
<--- Score

27. Is the need for organizational change recognized?
<--- Score

28. Why the need?
<--- Score

29. Think about the people you identified for your Cloud Database project and the project responsibilities you would assign to them, what kind of training do you think they would need to perform these responsibilities effectively?
<--- Score

30. Consider your own Cloud Database project, what types of organizational problems do you think might be causing or affecting your problem, based on the work done so far?
<--- Score

31. What is the recognized need?
<--- Score

32. Do you know what you need to know about Cloud Database?
<--- Score

33. What are the stakeholder objectives to be achieved with Cloud Database?

<--- Score

34. What problems are you facing and how do you consider Cloud Database will circumvent those obstacles?
<--- Score

35. How do you take a forward-looking perspective in identifying Cloud Database research related to market response and models?
<--- Score

36. How do you identify the kinds of information that you will need?
<--- Score

37. Are your goals realistic? Do you need to redefine your problem? Perhaps the problem has changed or maybe you have reached your goal and need to set a new one?
<--- Score

38. What vendors make products that address the Cloud Database needs?
<--- Score

39. Will Cloud Database deliverables need to be tested and, if so, by whom?
<--- Score

40. What extra resources will you need?
<--- Score

41. What needs to stay?
<--- Score

42. What tools and technologies are needed for a custom Cloud Database project?
<--- Score

43. What training and capacity building actions are needed to implement proposed reforms?
<--- Score

44. What activities does the governance board need to consider?
<--- Score

45. How many trainings, in total, are needed?
<--- Score

46. Will a response program recognize when a crisis occurs and provide some level of response?
<--- Score

47. What resources or support might you need?
<--- Score

48. Are employees recognized or rewarded for performance that demonstrates the highest levels of integrity?
<--- Score

49. Are there regulatory / compliance issues?
<--- Score

50. Is it clear when you think of the day ahead of you what activities and tasks you need to complete?
<--- Score

51. How much are sponsors, customers, partners, stakeholders involved in Cloud Database? In other

words, what are the risks, if Cloud Database does not deliver successfully?
<--- Score

52. Will new equipment/products be required to facilitate Cloud Database delivery, for example is new software needed?
<--- Score

53. What would happen if Cloud Database weren't done?
<--- Score

54. Are losses recognized in a timely manner?
<--- Score

55. What is the extent or complexity of the Cloud Database problem?
<--- Score

56. Have you identified your Cloud Database key performance indicators?
<--- Score

57. Do you need to avoid or amend any Cloud Database activities?
<--- Score

58. Which issues are too important to ignore?
<--- Score

59. Where do you need to exercise leadership?
<--- Score

60. What is the problem and/or vulnerability?
<--- Score

61. What do you need to start doing?
<--- Score

62. What Cloud Database events should you attend?
<--- Score

63. What are the timeframes required to resolve each of the issues/problems?
<--- Score

64. Are there recognized Cloud Database problems?
<--- Score

65. What prevents you from making the changes you know will make you a more effective Cloud Database leader?
<--- Score

66. Are there any specific expectations or concerns about the Cloud Database team, Cloud Database itself?
<--- Score

67. Which needs are not included or involved?
<--- Score

68. What are the expected benefits of Cloud Database to the stakeholder?
<--- Score

69. Who needs budgets?
<--- Score

70. Where is training needed?
<--- Score

71. What Cloud Database coordination do you need?
<--- Score

72. Are you dealing with any of the same issues today as yesterday? What can you do about this?
<--- Score

73. When a Cloud Database manager recognizes a problem, what options are available?
<--- Score

74. Would you recognize a threat from the inside?
<--- Score

75. What situation(s) led to this Cloud Database Self Assessment?
<--- Score

76. What is the smallest subset of the problem you can usefully solve?
<--- Score

77. For your Cloud Database project, identify and describe the business environment, is there more than one layer to the business environment?
<--- Score

78. How are training requirements identified?
<--- Score

79. Does your organization need more Cloud Database education?
<--- Score

80. Are problem definition and motivation clearly

presented?
<--- Score

81. What Cloud Database capabilities do you need?
<--- Score

82. What else needs to be measured?
<--- Score

83. Whom do you really need or want to serve?
<--- Score

84. What does Cloud Database success mean to the stakeholders?
<--- Score

85. What are your needs in relation to Cloud Database skills, labor, equipment, and markets?
<--- Score

86. Who should resolve the Cloud Database issues?
<--- Score

87. As a sponsor, customer or management, how important is it to meet goals, objectives?
<--- Score

88. Looking at each person individually – does every one have the qualities which are needed to work in this group?
<--- Score

89. Who else hopes to benefit from it?
<--- Score

90. How does it fit into your organizational needs and

tasks?

<--- Score

91. Are controls defined to recognize and contain problems?

<--- Score

92. What are the minority interests and what amount of minority interests can be recognized?

<--- Score

93. What are the Cloud Database resources needed?

<--- Score

94. How do you assess your Cloud Database workforce capability and capacity needs, including skills, competencies, and staffing levels?

<--- Score

Add up total points for this section:

_ _ _ _ _ = Total points for this section

Divided by: _ _ _ _ _ _ (number of statements answered) = _ _ _ _ _ _
Average score for this section

Transfer your score to the Cloud Database Index at the beginning of the Self-Assessment.

CRITERION #2: DEFINE:

INTENT: Formulate the stakeholder problem. Define the problem, needs and objectives.

In my belief, the answer to this question is clearly defined:

5 Strongly Agree

4 Agree

3 Neutral

2 Disagree

1 Strongly Disagree

1. What are the Cloud Database use cases?
<--- Score

2. Who is gathering Cloud Database information?
<--- Score

3. How do you build the right business case?
<--- Score

4. How would you define the culture at your organization, how susceptible is it to Cloud Database changes?
<--- Score

5. Has/have the customer(s) been identified?
<--- Score

6. What scope to assess?
<--- Score

7. Are audit criteria, scope, frequency and methods defined?
<--- Score

8. Has the direction changed at all during the course of Cloud Database? If so, when did it change and why?
<--- Score

9. What are the Cloud Database tasks and definitions?
<--- Score

10. How do you manage changes in Cloud Database requirements?
<--- Score

11. What is in the scope and what is not in scope?
<--- Score

12. What information should you gather?
<--- Score

13. What is a worst-case scenario for losses?
<--- Score

14. Who approved the Cloud Database scope?
<--- Score

15. Are accountability and ownership for Cloud Database clearly defined?
<--- Score

16. What are the rough order estimates on cost savings/opportunities that Cloud Database brings?
<--- Score

17. Are all requirements met?
<--- Score

18. In what way can you redefine the criteria of choice clients have in your category in your favor?
<--- Score

19. How do you catch Cloud Database definition inconsistencies?
<--- Score

20. What are the compelling stakeholder reasons for embarking on Cloud Database?
<--- Score

21. When is/was the Cloud Database start date?
<--- Score

22. Are different versions of process maps needed to account for the different types of inputs?
<--- Score

23. Has a high-level 'as is' process map been completed, verified and validated?
<--- Score

24. Is the current 'as is' process being followed? If not, what are the discrepancies?
<--- Score

25. Are resources adequate for the scope?
<--- Score

26. Is Cloud Database required?
<--- Score

27. What key stakeholder process output measure(s) does Cloud Database leverage and how?
<--- Score

28. What are the dynamics of the communication plan?
<--- Score

29. How do you keep key subject matter experts in the loop?
<--- Score

30. How do you gather the stories?
<--- Score

31. What system do you use for gathering Cloud Database information?
<--- Score

32. Has anyone else (internal or external to the group) attempted to solve this problem or a similar one before? If so, what knowledge can be leveraged from these previous efforts?
<--- Score

33. What is out of scope?
<--- Score

34. What gets examined?
<--- Score

35. Where can you gather more information?
<--- Score

36. What specifically is the problem? Where does it occur? When does it occur? What is its extent?
<--- Score

37. How have you defined all Cloud Database requirements first?
<--- Score

38. Is Cloud Database currently on schedule according to the plan?
<--- Score

39. What defines best in class?
<--- Score

40. Has a Cloud Database requirement not been met?
<--- Score

41. How do you manage scope?
<--- Score

42. What intelligence can you gather?
<--- Score

43. How do you manage unclear Cloud Database requirements?
<--- Score

44. What are the requirements for audit information?
<--- Score

45. What would be the goal or target for a Cloud Database's improvement team?
<--- Score

46. Have the customer needs been translated into specific, measurable requirements? How?
<--- Score

47. What Cloud Database services do you require?
<--- Score

48. What is in scope?
<--- Score

49. What was the context?
<--- Score

50. What is the scope of Cloud Database?
<--- Score

51. Is the Cloud Database scope complete and appropriately sized?
<--- Score

52. How do you gather Cloud Database requirements?
<--- Score

53. Are there different segments of customers?
<--- Score

54. Are the Cloud Database requirements complete?
<--- Score

55. Has the improvement team collected the 'voice of the customer' (obtained feedback – qualitative and quantitative)?
<--- Score

56. What is the definition of success?
<--- Score

57. The political context: who holds power?
<--- Score

58. Does the team have regular meetings?
<--- Score

59. When is the estimated completion date?
<--- Score

60. How do you think the partners involved in Cloud Database would have defined success?
<--- Score

61. What critical content must be communicated – who, what, when, where, and how?
<--- Score

62. Has your scope been defined?
<--- Score

63. How does the Cloud Database manager ensure against scope creep?
<--- Score

64. How did the Cloud Database manager receive input to the development of a Cloud Database improvement plan and the estimated completion

dates/times of each activity?
<--- Score

65. What are the record-keeping requirements of Cloud Database activities?
<--- Score

66. What customer feedback methods were used to solicit their input?
<--- Score

67. Do you have a Cloud Database success story or case study ready to tell and share?
<--- Score

68. How will variation in the actual durations of each activity be dealt with to ensure that the expected Cloud Database results are met?
<--- Score

69. Is the scope of Cloud Database defined?
<--- Score

70. Are required metrics defined, what are they?
<--- Score

71. Is the Cloud Database scope manageable?
<--- Score

72. What scope do you want your strategy to cover?
<--- Score

73. How do you gather requirements?
<--- Score

74. Is special Cloud Database user knowledge

required?
<--- Score

75. Have specific policy objectives been defined?
<--- Score

76. What constraints exist that might impact the team?
<--- Score

77. Scope of sensitive information?
<--- Score

78. How would you define Cloud Database leadership?
<--- Score

79. When are meeting minutes sent out? Who is on the distribution list?
<--- Score

80. What are the core elements of the Cloud Database business case?
<--- Score

81. How can the value of Cloud Database be defined?
<--- Score

82. What are (control) requirements for Cloud Database Information?
<--- Score

83. What are the tasks and definitions?
<--- Score

84. Are roles and responsibilities formally defined?

<--- Score

85. Are there any constraints known that bear on the ability to perform Cloud Database work? How is the team addressing them?
<--- Score

86. What happens if Cloud Database's scope changes?
<--- Score

87. What Cloud Database requirements should be gathered?
<--- Score

88. How is the team tracking and documenting its work?
<--- Score

89. What knowledge or experience is required?
<--- Score

90. What are the Roles and Responsibilities for each team member and its leadership? Where is this documented?
<--- Score

91. Do you all define Cloud Database in the same way?
<--- Score

92. Why are you doing Cloud Database and what is the scope?
<--- Score

93. Does the scope remain the same?
<--- Score

94. Is there any additional Cloud Database definition of success?
<--- Score

95. Has the Cloud Database work been fairly and/ or equitably divided and delegated among team members who are qualified and capable to perform the work? Has everyone contributed?
<--- Score

96. What is the scope of the Cloud Database effort?
<--- Score

97. Is scope creep really all bad news?
<--- Score

98. What information do you gather?
<--- Score

99. Are the Cloud Database requirements testable?
<--- Score

100. Is there regularly 100% attendance at the team meetings? If not, have appointed substitutes attended to preserve cross-functionality and full representation?
<--- Score

101. How often are the team meetings?
<--- Score

102. Is the work to date meeting requirements?
<--- Score

103. How are consistent Cloud Database definitions

important?

<--- Score

104. Have all of the relationships been defined properly?

<--- Score

105. What is the definition of Cloud Database excellence?

<--- Score

106. What baselines are required to be defined and managed?

<--- Score

107. What is the worst case scenario?

<--- Score

108. Is the team adequately staffed with the desired cross-functionality? If not, what additional resources are available to the team?

<--- Score

109. Has a team charter been developed and communicated?

<--- Score

110. What are the boundaries of the scope? What is in bounds and what is not? What is the start point? What is the stop point?

<--- Score

111. Is it clearly defined in and to your organization what you do?

<--- Score

112. What is out-of-scope initially?
<--- Score

113. Do the problem and goal statements meet the SMART criteria (specific, measurable, attainable, relevant, and time-bound)?
<--- Score

114. Is there a critical path to deliver Cloud Database results?
<--- Score

115. If substitutes have been appointed, have they been briefed on the Cloud Database goals and received regular communications as to the progress to date?
<--- Score

116. How and when will the baselines be defined?
<--- Score

117. Is the improvement team aware of the different versions of a process: what they think it is vs. what it actually is vs. what it should be vs. what it could be?
<--- Score

118. Do you have organizational privacy requirements?
<--- Score

119. Who is gathering information?
<--- Score

120. Are task requirements clearly defined?
<--- Score

121. Who defines (or who defined) the rules and roles?
<--- Score

122. How will the Cloud Database team and the group measure complete success of Cloud Database?
<--- Score

123. Are approval levels defined for contracts and supplements to contracts?
<--- Score

124. Has a project plan, Gantt chart, or similar been developed/completed?
<--- Score

125. Is Cloud Database linked to key stakeholder goals and objectives?
<--- Score

126. Will a Cloud Database production readiness review be required?
<--- Score

127. How do you hand over Cloud Database context?
<--- Score

128. How was the 'as is' process map developed, reviewed, verified and validated?
<--- Score

129. What sort of initial information to gather?
<--- Score

Add up total points for this section:
_ _ _ _ _ = Total points for this section

Divided by: _____ (number of
statements answered) = _____
Average score for this section

Transfer your score to the Cloud
Database Index at the beginning of the
Self-Assessment.

CRITERION #3: MEASURE:

INTENT: Gather the correct data. Measure the current performance and evolution of the situation.

In my belief, the answer to this question is clearly defined:

5 Strongly Agree

4 Agree

3 Neutral

2 Disagree

1 Strongly Disagree

1. How to cause the change?
<--- Score

2. How do you prevent mis-estimating cost?
<--- Score

3. How do you measure success?
<--- Score

4. What drives O&M cost?

<--- Score

5. What evidence is there and what is measured?

<--- Score

6. Are you able to realize any cost savings?

<--- Score

7. What are the strategic priorities for this year?

<--- Score

8. Do you have any cost Cloud Database limitation requirements?

<--- Score

9. What is an unallowable cost?

<--- Score

10. Does the Cloud Database task fit the client's priorities?

<--- Score

11. Why do you expend time and effort to implement measurement, for whom?

<--- Score

12. How do you measure lifecycle phases?

<--- Score

13. What are the costs?

<--- Score

14. How will costs be allocated?

<--- Score

15. What causes innovation to fail or succeed in your organization?
<--- Score

16. What are your operating costs?
<--- Score

17. How do you quantify and qualify impacts?
<--- Score

18. What is the root cause(s) of the problem?
<--- Score

19. How do your measurements capture actionable Cloud Database information for use in exceeding your customers expectations and securing your customers engagement?
<--- Score

20. What potential environmental factors impact the Cloud Database effort?
<--- Score

21. How do you control the overall costs of your work processes?
<--- Score

22. What disadvantage does this cause for the user?
<--- Score

23. How will success or failure be measured?
<--- Score

24. Are you taking your company in the direction of better and revenue or cheaper and cost?
<--- Score

25. What could cause you to change course?
<--- Score

26. Who should receive measurement reports?
<--- Score

27. What does losing customers cost your organization?
<--- Score

28. Have you made assumptions about the shape of the future, particularly its impact on your customers and competitors?
<--- Score

29. What could cause delays in the schedule?
<--- Score

30. How can you reduce the costs of obtaining inputs?
<--- Score

31. How long to keep data and how to manage retention costs?
<--- Score

32. Are there measurements based on task performance?
<--- Score

33. What are allowable costs?
<--- Score

34. How are measurements made?
<--- Score

35. What are the Cloud Database key cost drivers?
<--- Score

36. What are your key Cloud Database organizational performance measures, including key short and longer-term financial measures?
<--- Score

37. What harm might be caused?
<--- Score

38. What causes extra work or rework?
<--- Score

39. Are there competing Cloud Database priorities?
<--- Score

40. Which costs should be taken into account?
<--- Score

41. How sensitive must the Cloud Database strategy be to cost?
<--- Score

42. What is the total cost related to deploying Cloud Database, including any consulting or professional services?
<--- Score

43. What measurements are being captured?
<--- Score

44. Are the Cloud Database benefits worth its costs?
<--- Score

45. Are indirect costs charged to the Cloud Database

program?
<--- Score

46. What are hidden Cloud Database quality costs?
<--- Score

47. What are the operational costs after Cloud
Database deployment?
<--- Score

48. What is the Cloud Database business impact?
<--- Score

49. How will you measure success?
<--- Score

50. How do you verify the Cloud Database
requirements quality?
<--- Score

51. Do you have an issue in getting priority?
<--- Score

52. Are missed Cloud Database opportunities costing
your organization money?
<--- Score

53. What does your operating model cost?
<--- Score

54. What are the estimated costs of proposed
changes?
<--- Score

55. Are supply costs steady or fluctuating?
<--- Score

56. What are the current costs of the Cloud Database process?

<--- Score

57. What details are required of the Cloud Database cost structure?

<--- Score

58. How is progress measured?

<--- Score

59. How do you measure variability?

<--- Score

60. Has a cost center been established?

<--- Score

61. How is performance measured?

<--- Score

62. How can you measure Cloud Database in a systematic way?

<--- Score

63. Where is the cost?

<--- Score

64. What happens if cost savings do not materialize?

<--- Score

65. How do you verify and develop ideas and innovations?

<--- Score

66. How do you verify the authenticity of the data and

information used?
<--- Score

67. What do you measure and why?
<--- Score

68. Do the benefits outweigh the costs?
<--- Score

69. Will Cloud Database have an impact on current business continuity, disaster recovery processes and/ or infrastructure?
<--- Score

70. How will effects be measured?
<--- Score

71. Does a Cloud Database quantification method exist?
<--- Score

72. Have you included everything in your Cloud Database cost models?
<--- Score

73. What are the costs of delaying Cloud Database action?
<--- Score

74. What can be used to verify compliance?
<--- Score

75. Which measures and indicators matter?
<--- Score

76. When a disaster occurs, who gets priority?

<--- Score

77. How are costs allocated?
<--- Score

78. At what cost?
<--- Score

79. How can you measure the performance?
<--- Score

80. How do you measure efficient delivery of Cloud Database services?
<--- Score

81. What are the uncertainties surrounding estimates of impact?
<--- Score

82. What are the types and number of measures to use?
<--- Score

83. Is there an opportunity to verify requirements?
<--- Score

84. Are the measurements objective?
<--- Score

85. What users will be impacted?
<--- Score

86. Are you aware of what could cause a problem?
<--- Score

87. What is your Cloud Database quality cost

segregation study?
<--- Score

88. What are the costs of reform?
<--- Score

89. What is the total fixed cost?
<--- Score

90. Was a business case (cost/benefit) developed?
<--- Score

91. Have design-to-cost goals been established?
<--- Score

92. How can you manage cost down?
<--- Score

93. How will your organization measure success?
<--- Score

94. What does a Test Case verify?
<--- Score

95. Why do the measurements/indicators matter?
<--- Score

96. Is the cost worth the Cloud Database effort ?
<--- Score

97. What is measured? Why?
<--- Score

98. Did you tackle the cause or the symptom?
<--- Score

99. What do people want to verify?
<--- Score

100. Are the units of measure consistent?
<--- Score

101. How frequently do you track Cloud Database measures?
<--- Score

102. Do you aggressively reward and promote the people who have the biggest impact on creating excellent Cloud Database services/products?
<--- Score

103. What is the cause of any Cloud Database gaps?
<--- Score

104. What is the cost of rework?
<--- Score

105. When should you bother with diagrams?
<--- Score

106. What are the Cloud Database investment costs?
<--- Score

107. What relevant entities could be measured?
<--- Score

108. How will measures be used to manage and adapt?
<--- Score

109. How do you aggregate measures across priorities?

<--- Score

110. What causes investor action?
<--- Score

111. Are there any easy-to-implement alternatives to Cloud Database? Sometimes other solutions are available that do not require the cost implications of a full-blown project?
<--- Score

112. When are costs are incurred?
<--- Score

113. What would be a real cause for concern?
<--- Score

114. How much does it cost?
<--- Score

115. Does management have the right priorities among projects?
<--- Score

116. What are the costs and benefits?
<--- Score

117. Is the solution cost-effective?
<--- Score

118. How do you verify performance?
<--- Score

119. What are your primary costs, revenues, assets?
<--- Score

120. How can you reduce costs?
<--- Score

121. What measurements are possible, practicable and meaningful?
<--- Score

122. What is your decision requirements diagram?
<--- Score

123. Which Cloud Database impacts are significant?
<--- Score

124. Are Cloud Database vulnerabilities categorized and prioritized?
<--- Score

125. How will you measure your Cloud Database effectiveness?
<--- Score

126. What are your customers expectations and measures?
<--- Score

127. What methods are feasible and acceptable to estimate the impact of reforms?
<--- Score

128. Among the Cloud Database product and service cost to be estimated, which is considered hardest to estimate?
<--- Score

129. Is it possible to estimate the impact of unanticipated complexity such as wrong or failed

assumptions, feedback, etcetera on proposed reforms?
<--- Score

130. What would it cost to replace your technology?
<--- Score

Add up total points for this section:
_____ = Total points for this section

Divided by: _____ (number of statements answered) = _____
Average score for this section

Transfer your score to the Cloud Database Index at the beginning of the Self-Assessment.

CRITERION #4: ANALYZE:

INTENT: Analyze causes, assumptions and hypotheses.

In my belief, the answer to this question is clearly defined:

5 Strongly Agree

4 Agree

3 Neutral

2 Disagree

1 Strongly Disagree

1. Do you have the authority to produce the output?
<--- Score

2. What did the team gain from developing a sub-process map?
<--- Score

3. Is there any way to speed up the process?
<--- Score

4. What do you need to qualify?
<--- Score

5. What does the data say about the performance of the stakeholder process?
<--- Score

6. Were Pareto charts (or similar) used to portray the 'heavy hitters' (or key sources of variation)?
<--- Score

7. How difficult is it to qualify what Cloud Database ROI is?
<--- Score

8. How will the data be checked for quality?
<--- Score

9. What Cloud Database data should be collected?
<--- Score

10. What qualifications are needed?
<--- Score

11. What are the various tools or options available to migrate to cloud database services?
<--- Score

12. What tools were used to narrow the list of possible causes?
<--- Score

13. Do your contracts/agreements contain data security obligations?
<--- Score

14. What quality tools were used to get through the analyze phase?
<--- Score

15. Where can you get qualified talent today?
<--- Score

16. What were the crucial 'moments of truth' on the process map?
<--- Score

17. What internal processes need improvement?
<--- Score

18. How is the data gathered?
<--- Score

19. Was a cause-and-effect diagram used to explore the different types of causes (or sources of variation)?
<--- Score

20. Who owns what data?
<--- Score

21. Have the problem and goal statements been updated to reflect the additional knowledge gained from the analyze phase?
<--- Score

22. What qualifies as competition?
<--- Score

23. What Cloud Database data will be collected?
<--- Score

24. Who qualifies to gain access to data?

<--- Score

25. What are your key performance measures or indicators and in-process measures for the control and improvement of your Cloud Database processes?
<--- Score

26. Do you have practices and procedures in place in areas to manage cloud databases?
<--- Score

27. How is Cloud Database data gathered?
<--- Score

28. What were the financial benefits resulting from any 'ground fruit or low-hanging fruit' (quick fixes)?
<--- Score

29. What are the disruptive Cloud Database technologies that enable your organization to radically change your business processes?
<--- Score

30. Identify an operational issue in your organization, for example, could a particular task be done more quickly or more efficiently by Cloud Database?
<--- Score

31. How can risk management be tied procedurally to process elements?
<--- Score

32. How was the detailed process map generated, verified, and validated?
<--- Score

33. What is the oversight process?
<--- Score

34. Who will facilitate the team and process?
<--- Score

35. What is your organizations process which leads to recognition of value generation?
<--- Score

36. Think about some of the processes you undertake within your organization, which do you own?
<--- Score

37. What is the Value Stream Mapping?
<--- Score

38. How are outputs preserved and protected?
<--- Score

39. What are the Cloud Database design outputs?
<--- Score

40. Is the final output clearly identified?
<--- Score

41. Should you invest in industry-recognized qualifications?
<--- Score

42. How do your work systems and key work processes relate to and capitalize on your core competencies?
<--- Score

43. What are your Cloud Database processes?

<--- Score

44. Is data and process analysis, root cause analysis and quantifying the gap/opportunity in place?
<--- Score

45. What data is gathered?
<--- Score

46. What are your current levels and trends in key Cloud Database measures or indicators of product and process performance that are important to and directly serve your customers?
<--- Score

47. Do you understand your management processes today?
<--- Score

48. How do you implement and manage your work processes to ensure that they meet design requirements?
<--- Score

49. Is the performance gap determined?
<--- Score

50. What conclusions were drawn from the team's data collection and analysis? How did the team reach these conclusions?
<--- Score

51. A compounding model resolution with available relevant data can often provide insight towards a solution methodology; which Cloud Database models, tools and techniques are necessary?

<--- Score

52. What Cloud Database data do you gather or use now?
<--- Score

53. How do you determine whether your cloud database is supported by SAS?
<--- Score

54. What qualifications and skills do you need?
<--- Score

55. What data do you need to collect?
<--- Score

56. What Cloud Database metrics are outputs of the process?
<--- Score

57. What are your outputs?
<--- Score

58. Who is involved with workflow mapping?
<--- Score

59. Is the Cloud Database process severely broken such that a re-design is necessary?
<--- Score

60. Can you add value to the current Cloud Database decision-making process (largely qualitative) by incorporating uncertainty modeling (more quantitative)?
<--- Score

61. How do mission and objectives affect the Cloud Database processes of your organization?
<--- Score

62. How much data can be collected in the given timeframe?
<--- Score

63. Do staff qualifications match your project?
<--- Score

64. Is there an established change management process?
<--- Score

65. What are the revised rough estimates of the financial savings/opportunity for Cloud Database improvements?
<--- Score

66. Do your employees have the opportunity to do what they do best everyday?
<--- Score

67. What are evaluation criteria for the output?
<--- Score

68. Was a detailed process map created to amplify critical steps of the 'as is' stakeholder process?
<--- Score

69. What tools were used to generate the list of possible causes?
<--- Score

70. Is there a strict change management process?

<--- Score

71. Is the suppliers process defined and controlled?
<--- Score

72. What successful thing are you doing today that may be blinding you to new growth opportunities?
<--- Score

73. What are your current levels and trends in key measures or indicators of Cloud Database product and process performance that are important to and directly serve your customers? How do these results compare with the performance of your competitors and other organizations with similar offerings?
<--- Score

74. Do your leaders quickly bounce back from setbacks?
<--- Score

75. What Cloud Database data should be managed?
<--- Score

76. An organizationally feasible system request is one that considers the mission, goals and objectives of the organization, key questions are: is the Cloud Database solution request practical and will it solve a problem or take advantage of an opportunity to achieve company goals?
<--- Score

77. How do you measure the operational performance of your key work systems and processes, including productivity, cycle time, and other appropriate measures of process effectiveness, efficiency, and

innovation?

<--- Score

78. Record-keeping requirements flow from the records needed as inputs, outputs, controls and for transformation of a Cloud Database process, are the records needed as inputs to the Cloud Database process available?

<--- Score

79. Is the required Cloud Database data gathered?

<--- Score

80. How is the way you as the leader think and process information affecting your organizational culture?

<--- Score

81. How is the Cloud Database Value Stream Mapping managed?

<--- Score

82. Who is involved in the management review process?

<--- Score

83. How will the Cloud Database data be captured?

<--- Score

84. Who will gather what data?

<--- Score

85. Do several people in different organizational units assist with the Cloud Database process?

<--- Score

86. What output to create?

<--- Score

87. How do you use Cloud Database data and information to support organizational decision making and innovation?
<--- Score

88. How do you identify specific Cloud Database investment opportunities and emerging trends?
<--- Score

89. What systems/processes must you excel at?
<--- Score

90. How will corresponding data be collected?
<--- Score

91. Where is Cloud Database data gathered?
<--- Score

92. What qualifications do Cloud Database leaders need?
<--- Score

93. What is your organizations system for selecting qualified vendors?
<--- Score

94. What is the Cloud Database Driver?
<--- Score

95. What other jobs or tasks affect the performance of the steps in the Cloud Database process?
<--- Score

96. What, related to, Cloud Database processes does

your organization outsource?
<--- Score

97. How is data used for program management and improvement?
<--- Score

98. What are the processes for audit reporting and management?
<--- Score

99. Who gets your output?
<--- Score

100. What are your best practices for minimizing Cloud Database project risk, while demonstrating incremental value and quick wins throughout the Cloud Database project lifecycle?
<--- Score

101. How often will data be collected for measures?
<--- Score

102. Has data output been validated?
<--- Score

103. What will drive Cloud Database change?
<--- Score

104. How do you ensure that the Cloud Database opportunity is realistic?
<--- Score

105. What are the Cloud Database business drivers?
<--- Score

106. What are the best opportunities for value improvement?
<--- Score

107. What kind of crime could a potential new hire have committed that would not only not disqualify him/her from being hired by your organization, but would actually indicate that he/she might be a particularly good fit?
<--- Score

108. Are Cloud Database changes recognized early enough to be approved through the regular process?
<--- Score

109. How does the organization define, manage, and improve its Cloud Database processes?
<--- Score

110. What training and qualifications will you need?
<--- Score

111. What is the output?
<--- Score

112. Think about the functions involved in your Cloud Database project, what processes flow from these functions?
<--- Score

113. What is the cost of poor quality as supported by the team's analysis?
<--- Score

114. What types of data do your Cloud Database indicators require?

<--- Score

115. What process should you select for improvement?
<--- Score

116. How do you define collaboration and team output?
<--- Score

117. What are the personnel training and qualifications required?
<--- Score

118. What controls do you have in place to protect data?
<--- Score

119. What methods do you use to gather Cloud Database data?
<--- Score

120. When should a process be art not science?
<--- Score

121. What process improvements will be needed?
<--- Score

122. What other organizational variables, such as reward systems or communication systems, affect the performance of this Cloud Database process?
<--- Score

123. What qualifications are necessary?
<--- Score

124. Do you, as a leader, bounce back quickly from setbacks?

<--- Score

125. Were any designed experiments used to generate additional insight into the data analysis?

<--- Score

126. Are you missing Cloud Database opportunities?

<--- Score

127. Do quality systems drive continuous improvement?

<--- Score

128. Where is the data coming from to measure compliance?

<--- Score

129. What are the necessary qualifications?

<--- Score

130. How has the Cloud Database data been gathered?

<--- Score

131. Were there any improvement opportunities identified from the process analysis?

<--- Score

132. Which Cloud Database data should be retained?

<--- Score

133. Is the gap/opportunity displayed and communicated in financial terms?

<--- Score

134. What resources go in to get the desired output?
<--- Score

Add up total points for this section:
_____ = Total points for this section

Divided by: _____ (number of
statements answered) = _____
Average score for this section

Transfer your score to the Cloud
Database Index at the beginning of the
Self-Assessment.

CRITERION #5: IMPROVE:

INTENT: Develop a practical solution.
Innovate, establish and test the
solution and to measure the results.

In my belief, the answer to this
question is clearly defined:

5 Strongly Agree

4 Agree

3 Neutral

2 Disagree

1 Strongly Disagree

1. Are risk management tasks balanced centrally and locally?
<--- Score

2. How will you measure the results?
<--- Score

3. Is the solution technically practical?
<--- Score

4. What improvements have been achieved?
<--- Score

5. How do you decide how much to remunerate an employee?
<--- Score

6. Would you develop a Cloud Database Communication Strategy?
<--- Score

7. Do you combine technical expertise with business knowledge and Cloud Database Key topics include lifecycles, development approaches, requirements and how to make a business case?
<--- Score

8. What went well, what should change, what can improve?
<--- Score

9. If you could go back in time five years, what decision would you make differently? What is your best guess as to what decision you're making today you might regret five years from now?
<--- Score

10. To what extent does management recognize Cloud Database as a tool to increase the results?
<--- Score

11. In the past few months, what is the smallest change you have made that has had the biggest positive result? What was it about that small change that produced the large return?

<--- Score

12. How do you measure progress and evaluate training effectiveness?
<--- Score

13. What are the affordable Cloud Database risks?
<--- Score

14. Are you assessing Cloud Database and risk?
<--- Score

15. Is there a high likelihood that any recommendations will achieve their intended results?
<--- Score

16. What should a proof of concept or pilot accomplish?
<--- Score

17. How can you better manage risk?
<--- Score

18. Risk factors: what are the characteristics of Cloud Database that make it risky?
<--- Score

19. What is the implementation plan?
<--- Score

20. At what point will vulnerability assessments be performed once Cloud Database is put into production (e.g., ongoing Risk Management after implementation)?
<--- Score

21. What Cloud Database improvements can be made?
<--- Score

22. What error proofing will be done to address some of the discrepancies observed in the 'as is' process?
<--- Score

23. How does your organization evaluate strategic Cloud Database success?
<--- Score

24. How will you know that you have improved?
<--- Score

25. How are Cloud Database risks managed?
<--- Score

26. Who will be using the results of the measurement activities?
<--- Score

27. How do you link measurement and risk?
<--- Score

28. How do you manage Cloud Database risk?
<--- Score

29. How do you keep improving Cloud Database?
<--- Score

30. What resources are required for the improvement efforts?
<--- Score

31. How do you improve Cloud Database service

perception, and satisfaction?
<--- Score

32. Will the controls trigger any other risks?
<--- Score

33. What communications are necessary to support
the implementation of the solution?
<--- Score

34. How is knowledge sharing about risk
management improved?
<--- Score

35. What assumptions are made about the solution
and approach?
<--- Score

36. Where do you need Cloud Database
improvement?
<--- Score

37. What tools do you use once you have decided on
a Cloud Database strategy and more importantly how
do you choose?
<--- Score

38. What actually has to improve and by how much?
<--- Score

39. How significant is the improvement in the eyes of
the end user?
<--- Score

40. What does the 'should be' process map/design
look like?

<--- Score

41. What is the team's contingency plan for potential problems occurring in implementation?
<--- Score

42. Risk Identification: What are the possible risk events your organization faces in relation to Cloud Database?
<--- Score

43. Are decisions made in a timely manner?
<--- Score

44. What is the Cloud Database's sustainability risk?
<--- Score

45. Can the solution be designed and implemented within an acceptable time period?
<--- Score

46. How do you mitigate Cloud Database risk?
<--- Score

47. How do you improve productivity?
<--- Score

48. Who controls the risk?
<--- Score

49. Explorations of the frontiers of Cloud Database will help you build influence, improve Cloud Database, optimize decision making, and sustain change, what is your approach?
<--- Score

50. What tools were used to evaluate the potential solutions?
<--- Score

51. Are procedures documented for managing Cloud Database risks?
<--- Score

52. Was a Cloud Database charter developed?
<--- Score

53. What can you do to improve?
<--- Score

54. Is supporting Cloud Database documentation required?
<--- Score

55. Is the Cloud Database documentation thorough?
<--- Score

56. What lessons, if any, from a pilot were incorporated into the design of the full-scale solution?
<--- Score

57. Where do the Cloud Database decisions reside?
<--- Score

58. What tools were most useful during the improve phase?
<--- Score

59. What is the risk?
<--- Score

60. How will you recognize and celebrate results?

<--- Score

61. What are the concrete Cloud Database results?
<--- Score

62. Does the goal represent a desired result that can be measured?
<--- Score

63. Who should make the Cloud Database decisions?
<--- Score

64. What to do with the results or outcomes of measurements?
<--- Score

65. Can you integrate quality management and risk management?
<--- Score

66. Is Cloud Database documentation maintained?
<--- Score

67. Who makes the Cloud Database decisions in your organization?
<--- Score

68. What were the underlying assumptions on the cost-benefit analysis?
<--- Score

69. Does a good decision guarantee a good outcome?
<--- Score

70. How do you measure risk?
<--- Score

71. Who are the key stakeholders for the Cloud Database evaluation?
<--- Score

72. Have you identified breakpoints and/or risk tolerances that will trigger broad consideration of a potential need for intervention or modification of strategy?
<--- Score

73. How scalable is your Cloud Database solution?
<--- Score

74. How do you go about comparing Cloud Database approaches/solutions?
<--- Score

75. What are the Cloud Database security risks?
<--- Score

76. Were any criteria developed to assist the team in testing and evaluating potential solutions?
<--- Score

77. What area needs the greatest improvement?
<--- Score

78. How do you measure improved Cloud Database service perception, and satisfaction?
<--- Score

79. How do you deal with Cloud Database risk?
<--- Score

80. How do you improve your likelihood of success ?

<--- Score

81. Is there any other Cloud Database solution?
<--- Score

82. Are events managed to resolution?
<--- Score

83. What are your current levels and trends in key measures or indicators of workforce and leader development?
<--- Score

84. Which of the recognised risks out of all risks can be most likely transferred?
<--- Score

85. Have you achieved Cloud Database improvements?
<--- Score

86. Do vendor agreements bring new compliance risk ?
<--- Score

87. Can you identify any significant risks or exposures to Cloud Database third- parties (vendors, service providers, alliance partners etc) that concern you?
<--- Score

88. Do you need to do a usability evaluation?
<--- Score

89. What criteria will you use to assess your Cloud Database risks?
<--- Score

90. Who manages supplier risk management in your organization?
<--- Score

91. How is continuous improvement applied to risk management?
<--- Score

92. Cloud Database risk decisions: whose call Is It?
<--- Score

93. Is the Cloud Database risk managed?
<--- Score

94. What risks do you need to manage?
<--- Score

95. Who will be responsible for making the decisions to include or exclude requested changes once Cloud Database is underway?
<--- Score

96. How do you define the solutions' scope?
<--- Score

97. Which Cloud Database solution is appropriate?
<--- Score

98. What practices helps your organization to develop its capacity to recognize patterns?
<--- Score

99. How can skill-level changes improve Cloud Database?
<--- Score

100. What were the criteria for evaluating a Cloud
Database pilot?
<--- Score

101. Is the Cloud Database solution sustainable?
<--- Score

102. Who are the Cloud Database decision makers?
<--- Score

103. Who controls key decisions that will be made?
<--- Score

104. Who are the Cloud Database decision-makers?
<--- Score

105. What alternative responses are available to
manage risk?
<--- Score

106. How does the team improve its work?
<--- Score

107. What is Cloud Database risk?
<--- Score

108. Who will be responsible for documenting the
Cloud Database requirements in detail?
<--- Score

109. Is the measure of success for Cloud Database
understandable to a variety of people?
<--- Score

110. What are the implications of the one critical

Cloud Database decision 10 minutes, 10 months, and 10 years from now?
<--- Score

111. For decision problems, how do you develop a decision statement?
<--- Score

112. How are policy decisions made and where?
<--- Score

113. Are risk triggers captured?
<--- Score

114. How do you manage and improve your Cloud Database work systems to deliver customer value and achieve organizational success and sustainability?
<--- Score

115. What do you want to improve?
<--- Score

116. How can you improve performance?
<--- Score

117. How can you improve Cloud Database?
<--- Score

118. Why improve in the first place?
<--- Score

119. What tools were used to tap into the creativity and encourage 'outside the box' thinking?
<--- Score

120. What is the magnitude of the improvements?

<--- Score

121. Do those selected for the Cloud Database team have a good general understanding of what Cloud Database is all about?
<--- Score

122. Are the most efficient solutions problem-specific?
<--- Score

123. Who do you report Cloud Database results to?
<--- Score

124. How do the Cloud Database results compare with the performance of your competitors and other organizations with similar offerings?
<--- Score

125. Risk events: what are the things that could go wrong?
<--- Score

126. Do you have the optimal project management team structure?
<--- Score

127. For estimation problems, how do you develop an estimation statement?
<--- Score

128. How risky is your organization?
<--- Score

129. Is risk periodically assessed?
<--- Score

130. What is Cloud Database's impact on utilizing the best solution(s)?
<--- Score

131. What attendant changes will need to be made to ensure that the solution is successful?
<--- Score

132. Do you cover the five essential competencies: Communication, Collaboration,Innovation, Adaptability, and Leadership that improve an organizations ability to leverage the new Cloud Database in a volatile global economy?
<--- Score

133. What needs improvement? Why?
<--- Score

134. Are the key business and technology risks being managed?
<--- Score

135. Are the risks fully understood, reasonable and manageable?
<--- Score

136. What current systems have to be understood and/or changed?
<--- Score

Add up total points for this section:
_ _ _ _ _ = Total points for this section

Divided by: _ _ _ _ _ _ (number of statements answered) = _ _ _ _ _ _ Average score for this section

Transfer your score to the Cloud
Database Index at the beginning of the
Self-Assessment.

CRITERION #6: CONTROL:

INTENT: Implement the practical solution. Maintain the performance and correct possible complications.

In my belief, the answer to this question is clearly defined:

5 Strongly Agree

4 Agree

3 Neutral

2 Disagree

1 Strongly Disagree

1. What key inputs and outputs are being measured on an ongoing basis?
<--- Score

2. Who is the Cloud Database process owner?
<--- Score

3. What are the performance and scale of the Cloud Database tools?

<--- Score

4. Does a troubleshooting guide exist or is it needed?
<--- Score

5. Are pertinent alerts monitored, analyzed and distributed to appropriate personnel?
<--- Score

6. In the case of a Cloud Database project, the criteria for the audit derive from implementation objectives, an audit of a Cloud Database project involves assessing whether the recommendations outlined for implementation have been met, can you track that any Cloud Database project is implemented as planned, and is it working?
<--- Score

7. Does the response plan contain a definite closed loop continual improvement scheme (e.g., plan-do-check-act)?
<--- Score

8. What other systems, operations, processes, and infrastructures (hiring practices, staffing, training, incentives/rewards, metrics/dashboards/scorecards, etc.) need updates, additions, changes, or deletions in order to facilitate knowledge transfer and improvements?
<--- Score

9. Are the Cloud Database standards challenging?
<--- Score

10. Do the Cloud Database decisions you make today help people and the planet tomorrow?

<--- Score

11. Is the Cloud Database test/monitoring cost justified?
<--- Score

12. How do you select, collect, align, and integrate Cloud Database data and information for tracking daily operations and overall organizational performance, including progress relative to strategic objectives and action plans?
<--- Score

13. How will input, process, and output variables be checked to detect for sub-optimal conditions?
<--- Score

14. How will the process owner and team be able to hold the gains?
<--- Score

15. How likely is the current Cloud Database plan to come in on schedule or on budget?
<--- Score

16. How is change control managed?
<--- Score

17. Is there an action plan in case of emergencies?
<--- Score

18. Have new or revised work instructions resulted?
<--- Score

19. Who controls critical resources?
<--- Score

20. Do you monitor the Cloud Database decisions made and fine tune them as they evolve?
<--- Score

21. What do you measure to verify effectiveness gains?
<--- Score

22. Is there a standardized process?
<--- Score

23. How do you establish and deploy modified action plans if circumstances require a shift in plans and rapid execution of new plans?
<--- Score

24. Are you measuring, monitoring and predicting Cloud Database activities to optimize operations and profitability, and enhancing outcomes?
<--- Score

25. Who is going to spread your message?
<--- Score

26. What are the key elements of your Cloud Database performance improvement system, including your evaluation, organizational learning, and innovation processes?
<--- Score

27. Has the improved process and its steps been standardized?
<--- Score

28. What are you attempting to measure/monitor?

<--- Score

29. How will new or emerging customer needs/
requirements be checked/communicated to orient
the process toward meeting the new specifications
and continually reducing variation?
<--- Score

30. Are new process steps, standards, and
documentation ingrained into normal operations?
<--- Score

31. Are controls in place and consistently applied?
<--- Score

32. Are there documented procedures?
<--- Score

33. Will existing staff require re-training, for example,
to learn new business processes?
<--- Score

34. Does job training on the documented procedures
need to be part of the process team's education and
training?
<--- Score

35. Who will be in control?
<--- Score

36. How will you measure your QA plan's
effectiveness?
<--- Score

37. Who sets the Cloud Database standards?
<--- Score

38. What other areas of the group might benefit from the Cloud Database team's improvements, knowledge, and learning?
<--- Score

39. Is there a Cloud Database Communication plan covering who needs to get what information when?
<--- Score

40. Will the team be available to assist members in planning investigations?
<--- Score

41. You may have created your quality measures at a time when you lacked resources, technology wasn't up to the required standard, or low service levels were the industry norm. Have those circumstances changed?
<--- Score

42. What is the standard for acceptable Cloud Database performance?
<--- Score

43. How will the day-to-day responsibilities for monitoring and continual improvement be transferred from the improvement team to the process owner?
<--- Score

44. How do you monitor usage and cost?
<--- Score

45. What quality tools were useful in the control phase?

<--- Score

46. Are suggested corrective/restorative actions indicated on the response plan for known causes to problems that might surface?
<--- Score

47. What should you measure to verify efficiency gains?
<--- Score

48. Can you adapt and adjust to changing Cloud Database situations?
<--- Score

49. Act/Adjust: What Do you Need to Do Differently?
<--- Score

50. How do you encourage people to take control and responsibility?
<--- Score

51. Has the Cloud Database value of standards been quantified?
<--- Score

52. What are the known security controls?
<--- Score

53. How will the process owner verify improvement in present and future sigma levels, process capabilities?
<--- Score

54. Do the viable solutions scale to future needs?
<--- Score

55. Does Cloud Database appropriately measure and monitor risk?

<--- Score

56. Is there a transfer of ownership and knowledge to process owner and process team tasked with the responsibilities.

<--- Score

57. Will your goals reflect your program budget?

<--- Score

58. Is there a recommended audit plan for routine surveillance inspections of Cloud Database's gains?

<--- Score

59. Is a response plan in place for when the input, process, or output measures indicate an 'out-of-control' condition?

<--- Score

60. How do your controls stack up?

<--- Score

61. What is your theory of human motivation, and how does your compensation plan fit with that view?

<--- Score

62. Where do ideas that reach policy makers and planners as proposals for Cloud Database strengthening and reform actually originate?

<--- Score

63. What is the control/monitoring plan?

<--- Score

64. How can you best use all of your knowledge repositories to enhance learning and sharing?
<--- Score

65. What can you control?
<--- Score

66. What Cloud Database standards are applicable?
<--- Score

67. How do senior leaders actions reflect a commitment to the organizations Cloud Database values?
<--- Score

68. What is the best design framework for Cloud Database organization now that, in a post industrial-age if the top-down, command and control model is no longer relevant?
<--- Score

69. Is knowledge gained on process shared and institutionalized?
<--- Score

70. Is there a documented and implemented monitoring plan?
<--- Score

71. Can support from partners be adjusted?
<--- Score

72. What are the critical parameters to watch?
<--- Score

73. Is a response plan established and deployed?

<--- Score

74. Are the planned controls in place?
<--- Score

75. Does the Cloud Database performance meet the customer's requirements?
<--- Score

76. Against what alternative is success being measured?
<--- Score

77. How might the group capture best practices and lessons learned so as to leverage improvements?
<--- Score

78. What is the recommended frequency of auditing?
<--- Score

79. Are the planned controls working?
<--- Score

80. How will report readings be checked to effectively monitor performance?
<--- Score

81. What should the next improvement project be that is related to Cloud Database?
<--- Score

82. What do you stand for--and what are you against?
<--- Score

83. What adjustments to the strategies are needed?
<--- Score

84. What is your plan to assess your security risks?
<--- Score

85. How do you plan for the cost of succession?
<--- Score

86. How will Cloud Database decisions be made and monitored?
<--- Score

87. How is Cloud Database project cost planned, managed, monitored?
<--- Score

88. Who has control over resources?
<--- Score

89. How do controls support value?
<--- Score

90. Is there a control plan in place for sustaining improvements (short and long-term)?
<--- Score

91. How do you plan on providing proper recognition and disclosure of supporting companies?
<--- Score

92. Is new knowledge gained imbedded in the response plan?
<--- Score

93. Is there documentation that will support the successful operation of the improvement?
<--- Score

94. Are operating procedures consistent?
<--- Score

95. Are documented procedures clear and easy to follow for the operators?
<--- Score

96. What are customers monitoring?
<--- Score

97. How widespread is its use?
<--- Score

98. Is reporting being used or needed?
<--- Score

99. Will any special training be provided for results interpretation?
<--- Score

100. What are your results for key measures or indicators of the accomplishment of your Cloud Database strategy and action plans, including building and strengthening core competencies?
<--- Score

Add up total points for this section:
_ _ _ _ _ = Total points for this section

Divided by: _ _ _ _ _ _ (number of statements answered) = _ _ _ _ _ _
Average score for this section

Transfer your score to the Cloud Database Index at the beginning of the

Self-Assessment.

CRITERION #7: SUSTAIN:

INTENT: Retain the benefits.

In my belief, the answer to this question is clearly defined:

5 Strongly Agree

4 Agree

3 Neutral

2 Disagree

1 Strongly Disagree

1. Do you know what you are doing? And who do you call if you don't?
<--- Score

2. Are the assumptions believable and achievable?
<--- Score

3. Who will manage the integration of tools?
<--- Score

4. Do you see more potential in people than they do

in themselves?
<--- Score

5. How is implementation research currently incorporated into each of your goals?
<--- Score

6. What counts that you are not counting?
<--- Score

7. Operational - will it work?
<--- Score

8. What are strategies for increasing support and reducing opposition?
<--- Score

9. If your customer were your grandmother, would you tell her to buy what you're selling?
<--- Score

10. How do you know if you are successful?
<--- Score

11. How do you assess the Cloud Database pitfalls that are inherent in implementing it?
<--- Score

12. Is a Cloud Database breakthrough on the horizon?
<--- Score

13. What is the recommended frequency of auditing?
<--- Score

14. What are the rules and assumptions your industry operates under? What if the opposite were true?

<--- Score

15. What is your Cloud Database strategy?
<--- Score

16. Do you say no to customers for no reason?
<--- Score

17. Can you do all this work?
<--- Score

18. What are specific Cloud Database rules to follow?
<--- Score

19. Who do we want your customers to become?
<--- Score

20. Do you have past Cloud Database successes?
<--- Score

21. What Cloud Database modifications can you make work for you?
<--- Score

22. What happens at your organization when people fail?
<--- Score

23. What are the challenges?
<--- Score

24. How are you doing compared to your industry?
<--- Score

25. Do you have the right capabilities and capacities?
<--- Score

26. How do you determine the key elements that affect Cloud Database workforce satisfaction, how are these elements determined for different workforce groups and segments?
<--- Score

27. If your company went out of business tomorrow, would anyone who doesn't get a paycheck here care?
<--- Score

28. Marketing budgets are tighter, consumers are more skeptical, and social media has changed forever the way we talk about Cloud Database, how do you gain traction?
<--- Score

29. In the past year, what have you done (or could you have done) to increase the accurate perception of your company/brand as ethical and honest?
<--- Score

30. How much does Cloud Database help?
<--- Score

31. What is a feasible sequencing of reform initiatives over time?
<--- Score

32. Do you have the right people on the bus?
<--- Score

33. Are all key stakeholders present at all Structured Walkthroughs?
<--- Score

34. How important is Cloud Database to the user organizations mission?
<--- Score

35. What is your competitive advantage?
<--- Score

36. Why will customers want to buy your organizations products/services?
<--- Score

37. Why should you adopt a Cloud Database framework?
<--- Score

38. How do you transition from the baseline to the target?
<--- Score

39. Is there a work around that you can use?
<--- Score

40. What is the estimated value of the project?
<--- Score

41. How can you become the company that would put you out of business?
<--- Score

42. Can you break it down?
<--- Score

43. Are your responses positive or negative?
<--- Score

44. Who is responsible for Cloud Database?

<--- Score

45. What have been your experiences in defining long range Cloud Database goals?
<--- Score

46. What relationships among Cloud Database trends do you perceive?
<--- Score

47. How do customers see your organization?
<--- Score

48. Will it be accepted by users?
<--- Score

49. What business benefits will Cloud Database goals deliver if achieved?
<--- Score

50. How do you keep the momentum going?
<--- Score

51. Is your strategy driving your strategy? Or is the way in which you allocate resources driving your strategy?
<--- Score

52. Do you have enough freaky customers in your portfolio pushing you to the limit day in and day out?
<--- Score

53. What is the purpose of Cloud Database in relation to the mission?
<--- Score

54. How do you govern and fulfill your societal responsibilities?
<--- Score

55. If you do not follow, then how to lead?
<--- Score

56. What potential megatrends could make your business model obsolete?
<--- Score

57. What happens when a new employee joins the organization?
<--- Score

58. What new services of functionality will be implemented next with Cloud Database ?
<--- Score

59. What stupid rule would you most like to kill?
<--- Score

60. When information truly is ubiquitous, when reach and connectivity are completely global, when computing resources are infinite, and when a whole new set of impossibilities are not only possible, but happening, what will that do to your business?
<--- Score

61. What unique value proposition (UVP) do you offer?
<--- Score

62. How do you track customer value, profitability or financial return, organizational success, and sustainability?
<--- Score

63. What are the barriers to increased Cloud Database production?
<--- Score

64. What are the business goals Cloud Database is aiming to achieve?
<--- Score

65. What will be the consequences to the stakeholder (financial, reputation etc) if Cloud Database does not go ahead or fails to deliver the objectives?
<--- Score

66. Do you feel that more should be done in the Cloud Database area?
<--- Score

67. What are internal and external Cloud Database relations?
<--- Score

68. How can you negotiate Cloud Database successfully with a stubborn boss, an irate client, or a deceitful coworker?
<--- Score

69. What are you challenging?
<--- Score

70. Are you using a design thinking approach and integrating Innovation, Cloud Database Experience, and Brand Value?
<--- Score

71. Which functions and people interact with the

supplier and or customer?
<--- Score

72. What is the range of capabilities?
<--- Score

73. What have you done to protect your business from competitive encroachment?
<--- Score

74. What trouble can you get into?
<--- Score

75. Who is responsible for errors?
<--- Score

76. How do you maintain Cloud Database's Integrity?
<--- Score

77. Do you have an implicit bias for capital investments over people investments?
<--- Score

78. Why should people listen to you?
<--- Score

79. Can you maintain your growth without detracting from the factors that have contributed to your success?
<--- Score

80. What must you excel at?
<--- Score

81. How will you know that the Cloud Database project has been successful?

<--- Score

82. What management system can you use to leverage the Cloud Database experience, ideas, and concerns of the people closest to the work to be done?
<--- Score

83. What does your signature ensure?
<--- Score

84. Is Cloud Database dependent on the successful delivery of a current project?
<--- Score

85. What role does communication play in the success or failure of a Cloud Database project?
<--- Score

86. If you find that you havent accomplished one of the goals for one of the steps of the Cloud Database strategy, what will you do to fix it?
<--- Score

87. Is there any reason to believe the opposite of my current belief?
<--- Score

88. Who are the key stakeholders?
<--- Score

89. What is your BATNA (best alternative to a negotiated agreement)?
<--- Score

90. Why do and why don't your customers like your

organization?

<--- Score

91. How do you cross-sell and up-sell your Cloud Database success?

<--- Score

92. Do you think you know, or do you know you know ?

<--- Score

93. What knowledge, skills and characteristics mark a good Cloud Database project manager?

<--- Score

94. What is something you believe that nearly no one agrees with you on?

<--- Score

95. Who is responsible for ensuring appropriate resources (time, people and money) are allocated to Cloud Database?

<--- Score

96. How can you incorporate support to ensure safe and effective use of Cloud Database into the services that you provide?

<--- Score

97. In a project to restructure Cloud Database outcomes, which stakeholders would you involve?

<--- Score

98. What is your formula for success in Cloud Database ?

<--- Score

99. Where can you break convention?
<--- Score

100. Why not do Cloud Database?
<--- Score

101. Did your employees make progress today?
<--- Score

102. What one word do you want to own in the minds of your customers, employees, and partners?
<--- Score

103. What you are going to do to affect the numbers?
<--- Score

104. Are you making progress, and are you making progress as Cloud Database leaders?
<--- Score

105. What are the potential basics of Cloud Database fraud?
<--- Score

106. Is a Cloud Database team work effort in place?
<--- Score

107. What are the gaps in your knowledge and experience?
<--- Score

108. Why is Cloud Database important for you now?
<--- Score

109. What are the essentials of internal Cloud

Database management?
<--- Score

110. Political -is anyone trying to undermine this project?
<--- Score

111. Who will be responsible for deciding whether Cloud Database goes ahead or not after the initial investigations?
<--- Score

112. Who, on the executive team or the board, has spoken to a customer recently?
<--- Score

113. How do you make it meaningful in connecting Cloud Database with what users do day-to-day?
<--- Score

114. If you got fired and a new hire took your place, what would she do different?
<--- Score

115. What is the craziest thing you can do?
<--- Score

116. What are the key enablers to make this Cloud Database move?
<--- Score

117. Will there be any necessary staff changes (redundancies or new hires)?
<--- Score

118. What are the short and long-term Cloud

Database goals?

<--- Score

119. What happens if you do not have enough funding?

<--- Score

120. What information is critical to your organization that your executives are ignoring?

<--- Score

121. If you had to rebuild your organization without any traditional competitive advantages (i.e., no killer technology, promising research, innovative product/service delivery model, etcetera), how would your people have to approach their work and collaborate together in order to create the necessary conditions for success?

<--- Score

122. How do you manage Cloud Database Knowledge Management (KM)?

<--- Score

123. What are the top 3 things at the forefront of your Cloud Database agendas for the next 3 years?

<--- Score

124. Who is on the team?

<--- Score

125. What are the usability implications of Cloud Database actions?

<--- Score

126. Do you know who is a friend or a foe?

<--- Score

127. Is there any existing Cloud Database governance structure?
<--- Score

128. Who will provide the final approval of Cloud Database deliverables?
<--- Score

129. Who uses your product in ways you never expected?
<--- Score

130. What are the long-term Cloud Database goals?
<--- Score

131. How do you foster innovation?
<--- Score

132. How do you stay inspired?
<--- Score

133. Is Cloud Database realistic, or are you setting yourself up for failure?
<--- Score

134. Who are your customers?
<--- Score

135. If you had to leave your organization for a year and the only communication you could have with employees/colleagues was a single paragraph, what would you write?
<--- Score

136. What could happen if you do not do it?
<--- Score

137. To whom do you add value?
<--- Score

138. What is the source of the strategies for Cloud Database strengthening and reform?
<--- Score

139. Who have you, as a company, historically been when you've been at your best?
<--- Score

140. Who else should you help?
<--- Score

141. Think of your Cloud Database project, what are the main functions?
<--- Score

142. What is effective Cloud Database?
<--- Score

143. If you were responsible for initiating and implementing major changes in your organization, what steps might you take to ensure acceptance of those changes?
<--- Score

144. How long will it take to change?
<--- Score

145. What are your most important goals for the strategic Cloud Database objectives?
<--- Score

146. Have new benefits been realized?
<--- Score

147. How much contingency will be available in the budget?
<--- Score

148. Whom among your colleagues do you trust, and for what?
<--- Score

149. Instead of going to current contacts for new ideas, what if you reconnected with dormant contacts--the people you used to know? If you were going reactivate a dormant tie, who would it be?
<--- Score

150. How do you create buy-in?
<--- Score

151. What did you miss in the interview for the worst hire you ever made?
<--- Score

152. How does Cloud Database integrate with other stakeholder initiatives?
<--- Score

153. What threat is Cloud Database addressing?
<--- Score

154. Whose voice (department, ethnic group, women, older workers, etc) might you have missed hearing from in your company, and how might you amplify this voice to create positive momentum for your

business?
<--- Score

155. Are you relevant? Will you be relevant five years from now? Ten?
<--- Score

156. Are you paying enough attention to the partners your company depends on to succeed?
<--- Score

157. What goals did you miss?
<--- Score

158. What are current Cloud Database paradigms?
<--- Score

159. What is the kind of project structure that would be appropriate for your Cloud Database project, should it be formal and complex, or can it be less formal and relatively simple?
<--- Score

160. What projects are going on in the organization today, and what resources are those projects using from the resource pools?
<--- Score

161. Do Cloud Database rules make a reasonable demand on a users capabilities?
<--- Score

162. How do you proactively clarify deliverables and Cloud Database quality expectations?
<--- Score

163. Are you satisfied with your current role? If not, what is missing from it?
<--- Score

164. What is the funding source for this project?
<--- Score

165. What may be the consequences for the performance of an organization if all stakeholders are not consulted regarding Cloud Database?
<--- Score

166. Which Cloud Database goals are the most important?
<--- Score

167. Is the impact that Cloud Database has shown?
<--- Score

168. Who will determine interim and final deadlines?
<--- Score

169. How do you set Cloud Database stretch targets and how do you get people to not only participate in setting these stretch targets but also that they strive to achieve these?
<--- Score

170. Can the schedule be done in the given time?
<--- Score

171. What would have to be true for the option on the table to be the best possible choice?
<--- Score

172. How do you listen to customers to obtain

actionable information?
<--- Score

173. Ask yourself: how would you do this work if you only had one staff member to do it?
<--- Score

174. What is an unauthorized commitment?
<--- Score

175. Have benefits been optimized with all key stakeholders?
<--- Score

176. What would you recommend your friend do if he/she were facing this dilemma?
<--- Score

177. What is it like to work for you?
<--- Score

178. How can you become more high-tech but still be high touch?
<--- Score

179. If no one would ever find out about your accomplishments, how would you lead differently?
<--- Score

180. What was the last experiment you ran?
<--- Score

181. Why is it important to have senior management support for a Cloud Database project?
<--- Score

182. What Cloud Database skills are most important?
<--- Score

183. How do you foster the skills, knowledge, talents, attributes, and characteristics you want to have?
<--- Score

184. Which models, tools and techniques are necessary?
<--- Score

185. What should you stop doing?
<--- Score

186. How do you ensure that implementations of Cloud Database products are done in a way that ensures safety?
<--- Score

187. How do you deal with Cloud Database changes?
<--- Score

188. Who do you want your customers to become?
<--- Score

189. Are assumptions made in Cloud Database stated explicitly?
<--- Score

190. What trophy do you want on your mantle?
<--- Score

191. If you weren't already in this business, would you enter it today? And if not, what are you going to do about it?
<--- Score

192. Is it economical; do you have the time and money?
<--- Score

193. Are you maintaining a past–present–future perspective throughout the Cloud Database discussion?
<--- Score

194. What is your question? Why?
<--- Score

195. What are your personal philosophies regarding Cloud Database and how do they influence your work?
<--- Score

196. Which individuals, teams or departments will be involved in Cloud Database?
<--- Score

197. Is your basic point _____ or _____?
<--- Score

198. Are you / should you be revolutionary or evolutionary?
<--- Score

199. Who are four people whose careers you have enhanced?
<--- Score

200. How do senior leaders deploy your organizations vision and values through your leadership system, to the workforce, to key suppliers and partners, and to

customers and other stakeholders, as appropriate?
<--- Score

201. What is the overall business strategy?
<--- Score

202. Do you think Cloud Database accomplishes the goals you expect it to accomplish?
<--- Score

203. What are you trying to prove to yourself, and how might it be hijacking your life and business success?
<--- Score

204. How do you engage the workforce, in addition to satisfying them?
<--- Score

205. What do we do when new problems arise?
<--- Score

206. Who is the main stakeholder, with ultimate responsibility for driving Cloud Database forward?
<--- Score

207. Are new benefits received and understood?
<--- Score

208. Is maximizing Cloud Database protection the same as minimizing Cloud Database loss?
<--- Score

209. Were lessons learned captured and communicated?
<--- Score

210. How likely is it that a customer would recommend your company to a friend or colleague?
<--- Score

211. How do you lead with Cloud Database in mind?
<--- Score

212. Is the Cloud Database organization completing tasks effectively and efficiently?
<--- Score

213. Would you rather sell to knowledgeable and informed customers or to uninformed customers?
<--- Score

Add up total points for this section:
_____ = Total points for this section

Divided by: _____ (number of statements answered) = _____
Average score for this section

Transfer your score to the Cloud Database Index at the beginning of the Self-Assessment.

Cloud Database and Managing Projects, Criteria for Project Managers:

1.0 Initiating Process Group: Cloud Database

1. Contingency planning. if a risk event occurs, what will you do?

2. The Cloud Database project managers have maximum authority in which type of organization?

3. What were things that you did well, and could improve, and how?

4. When are the deliverables to be generated in each phase?

5. Did the Cloud Database project team have the right skills?

6. Do you know all the stakeholders impacted by the Cloud Database project and what needs are?

7. Who are the Cloud Database project stakeholders?

8. Did the Cloud Database project team have the right skills?

9. How will you do it?

10. What will be the pressing issues of tomorrow?

11. Have you evaluated the teams performance and asked for feedback?

12. How well did the chosen processes produce the expected results?

13. Do you know if the Cloud Database project requires outside equipment or vendor resources?

14. Specific - is the objective clear in terms of what, how, when, and where the situation will be changed?

15. Are there resources to maintain and support the outcome of the Cloud Database project?

16. Will the Cloud Database project meet the client requirements, and will it achieve the business success criteria that justified doing the Cloud Database project in the first place?

17. Were resources available as planned?

18. What is the stake of others in your Cloud Database project?

19. How well did you do?

20. What are the overarching issues of your organization?

1.1 Project Charter: Cloud Database

21. Where does all this information come from?

22. Why executive support?

23. How will you learn more about the process or system you are trying to improve?

24. What material?

25. Success determination factors: how will the success of the Cloud Database project be determined from the customers perspective?

26. Who are the stakeholders?

27. Why have you chosen the aim you have set forth?

28. Why Outsource?

29. Dependent Cloud Database projects: what Cloud Database projects must be underway or completed before this Cloud Database project can be successful?

30. What does it need to do?

31. Is it an improvement over existing products?

32. What are some examples of a business case?

33. What is in it for you?

34. What is the justification?

35. How much?

36. Why do you need to manage scope?

37. Why the improvements?

38. How do you manage integration?

39. Pop quiz – which are the same inputs as in the Cloud Database project charter?

40. Assumptions: what factors, for planning purposes, are you considering to be true?

1.2 Stakeholder Register: Cloud Database

41. What are the major Cloud Database project milestones requiring communications or providing communications opportunities?

42. Is your organization ready for change?

43. How much influence do they have on the Cloud Database project?

44. How will reports be created?

45. Who is managing stakeholder engagement?

46. What opportunities exist to provide communications?

47. How big is the gap?

48. Who wants to talk about Security?

49. How should employers make voices heard?

50. What is the power of the stakeholder?

51. What & Why?

1.3 Stakeholder Analysis Matrix: Cloud Database

52. Processes and systems, etc?

53. Participatory approach: how will key stakeholders participate in the Cloud Database project?

54. Who has been involved in the area (thematic or geographic) in the past?

55. Do recommendations include actions to address any differential distribution of impacts?

56. Where are mitigation costs factored in?

57. What makes a person a stakeholder?

58. What advantages do your organizations stakeholders have?

59. How much do resources cost?

60. Are there two or three that rise to the top, and a couple that are sliding to the bottom?

61. What do you Evaluate?

62. Guiding question: what is the issue at stake?

63. How will the stakeholder directly benefit from the Cloud Database project and how will this affect the stakeholders motivation?

64. Identify the stakeholders levels most frequently used –or at least sought– in your Cloud Database projects and for which purpose?

65. Geographical, export, import?

66. Who will be affected by the Cloud Database project?

67. If the baseline is now, and if its improved it will be better than now?

68. Resource providers; who can provide resources to ensure the implementation of the Cloud Database project?

69. How do rules, behaviors affect stakes?

70. Processes, systems, it, communications?

71. Is there a clear description of the scope of practice of the Cloud Database projects educators?

2.0 Planning Process Group: Cloud Database

72. Cloud Database project assessment; why did you do this Cloud Database project?

73. Are the follow-up indicators relevant and do they meet the quality needed to measure the outputs and outcomes of the Cloud Database project?

74. Are you just doing busywork to pass the time?

75. When developing the estimates for Cloud Database project phases, you choose to add the individual estimates for the activities that comprise each phase. What type of estimation method are you using?

76. What good practices or successful experiences or transferable examples have been identified?

77. To what extent is the program helping to influence your organizations policy framework?

78. You did your readings, yes?

79. What types of differentiated effects are resulting from the Cloud Database project and to what extent?

80. In what ways can the governance of the Cloud Database project be improved so that it has greater likelihood of achieving future sustainability?

81. The Cloud Database project charter is created in which Cloud Database project management process group?

82. Why do it Cloud Database projects fail?

83. Just how important is your work to the overall success of the Cloud Database project?

84. To what extent are the visions and actions of the partners consistent or divergent with regard to the program?

85. How are the principles of aid effectiveness (ownership, alignment, management for development results and mutual responsibility) being applied in the Cloud Database project?

86. Who are the Cloud Database project stakeholders?

87. What are the different approaches to building the WBS?

88. What factors are contributing to progress or delay in the achievement of products and results?

89. In which Cloud Database project management process group is the detailed Cloud Database project budget created?

90. Mitigate. what will you do to minimize the impact should a risk event occur?

91. In what way has the Cloud Database project come up with innovative measures for problem-solving?

2.1 Project Management Plan: Cloud Database

92. Do the proposed changes from the Cloud Database project include any significant risks to safety?

93. Are the existing and future without-plan conditions reasonable and appropriate?

94. What is risk management?

95. Are there any Client staffing expectations?

96. Are alternatives safe, functional, constructible, economical, reasonable and sustainable?

97. What are the assigned resources?

98. Is there anything you would now do differently on your Cloud Database project based on past experience?

99. If the Cloud Database project is complex or scope is specialized, do you have appropriate and/or qualified staff available to perform the tasks?

100. Why Change?

101. How well are you able to manage your risk?

102. Who is the Cloud Database project Manager?

103. What are the known stakeholder requirements?

104. Is the budget realistic?

105. What are the assumptions?

106. Do there need to be organizational changes?

107. What would you do differently?

108. What would you do differently what did not work?

109. What should you drop in order to add something new?

2.2 Scope Management Plan: Cloud Database

110. How relevant is this attribute to this Cloud Database project or audit?

111. Staffing Requirements?

112. Have the procedures for identifying budget variances been followed?

113. Do Cloud Database project managers participating in the Cloud Database project know the Cloud Database projects true status first hand?

114. Can each item be appropriately scheduled?

115. Are Cloud Database project team members involved in detailed estimating and scheduling?

116. Are agendas created for each meeting with meeting objectives, meeting topics, invitee list, and action items from past meetings?

117. Are target dates established for each milestone deliverable?

118. Are there checklists created to demine if all quality processes are followed?

119. Are measurements and feedback mechanisms incorporated in tracking work effort & refining work estimating techniques?

120. Which statement about customer expectations is not true?

121. What weaknesses do you have?

122. What happens to rejected deliverables?

123. How do you know when you are finished?

124. Personnel with expertise?

125. The greatest degree of uncertainty is encountered during which phase of the Cloud Database project life cycle?

126. Describe the process for rejecting the Cloud Database project deliverables. What happens to rejected deliverables?

127. Is the Cloud Database project sponsor clearly communicating the business case or rationale for why this Cloud Database project is needed?

128. Are all key components of a Quality Assurance Plan present?

129. What are the risks that could significantly affect the scope of the Cloud Database project?

2.3 Requirements Management Plan: Cloud Database

130. Will you have access to stakeholders when you need them?

131. What are you counting on?

132. After the requirements are gathered and set forth on the requirements register, theyre little more than a laundry list of items. Some may be duplicates, some might conflict with others and some will be too broad or too vague to understand. Describe how the requirements will be analyzed. Who will perform the analysis?

133. Will the product release be stable and mature enough to be deployed in the user community?

134. When and how will a requirements baseline be established in this Cloud Database project?

135. Business analysis scope?

136. Will you perform a Requirements Risk assessment and develop a plan to deal with risks?

137. Who will do the reporting and to whom will reports be delivered?

138. How will you develop the schedule of requirements activities?

139. Have stakeholders been instructed in the Change Control process?

140. Describe the process for rejecting the Cloud Database project requirements. Who has the authority to reject Cloud Database project requirements?

141. How will bidders price evaluations be done, by deliverables, phases, or in a big bang?

142. Do you expect stakeholders to be cooperative?

143. To see if a requirement statement is sufficiently well-defined, read it from the developers perspective. Mentally add the phrase, call me when youre done to the end of the requirement and see if that makes you nervous. In other words, would you need additional clarification from the author to understand the requirement well enough to design and implement it?

144. Do you really need to write this document at all?

145. How will you communicate scheduled tasks to other team members?

146. Did you distinguish the scope of work the contractor(s) will be required to do?

147. Do you understand the role that each stakeholder will play in the requirements process?

148. Are actual resources expenditures versus planned expenditures acceptable?

149. Do you have an agreed upon process for alerting the Cloud Database project Manager if a request for

change in requirements leads to a product scope change?

2.4 Requirements Documentation: Cloud Database

150. Does the system provide the functions which best support the customers needs?

151. What are the attributes of a customer?

152. If applicable; are there issues linked with the fact that this is an offshore Cloud Database project?

153. Where do system and software requirements come from, what are sources?

154. What are the acceptance criteria?

155. Completeness. are all functions required by the customer included?

156. How linear / iterative is your Requirements Gathering process (or will it be)?

157. Can you check system requirements?

158. How can you document system requirements?

159. What will be the integration problems?

160. What are the potential disadvantages/ advantages?

161. What can tools do for us?

162. Who is interacting with the system?

163. Basic work/business process; high-level, what is being touched?

164. What is the risk associated with the technology?

165. The problem with gathering requirements is right there in the word gathering. What images does it conjure?

166. What is your Elevator Speech?

167. How does what is being described meet the business need?

168. Do technical resources exist?

169. Validity. does the system provide the functions which best support the customers needs?

2.5 Requirements Traceability Matrix: Cloud Database

170. What percentage of Cloud Database projects are producing traceability matrices between requirements and other work products?

171. How small is small enough?

172. Why do you manage scope?

173. Why use a WBS?

174. How will it affect the stakeholders personally in career?

175. Is there a requirements traceability process in place?

176. Will you use a Requirements Traceability Matrix?

177. What are the chronologies, contingencies, consequences, criteria?

178. Describe the process for approving requirements so they can be added to the traceability matrix and Cloud Database project work can be performed. Will the Cloud Database project requirements become approved in writing?

179. Do you have a clear understanding of all subcontracts in place?

180. What is the WBS?

181. How do you manage scope?

2.6 Project Scope Statement: Cloud Database

182. How often will scope changes be reviewed?

183. What is a process you might recommend to verify the accuracy of the research deliverable?

184. Did your Cloud Database project ask for this?

185. Will all Cloud Database project issues be unconditionally tracked through the issue resolution process?

186. Which risks does the Cloud Database project focus on?

187. Has the format for tracking and monitoring schedules and costs been defined?

188. Are there backup strategies for key members of the Cloud Database project?

189. Are the meetings set up to have assigned note takers that will add action/issues to the issue list?

190. What are the possible consequences should a risk come to occur?

191. Is there a process (test plans, inspections, reviews) defined for verifying outputs for each task?

192. Any new risks introduced or old risks impacted.

Are there issues that could affect the existing requirements for the result, service, or product if the scope changes?

193. Where and how does the team fit within your organization structure?

194. Cloud Database project lead, team lead, solution architect?

195. Is the plan for your organization of the Cloud Database project resources adequate?

196. What are the major deliverables of the Cloud Database project?

197. Is the plan for Cloud Database project resources adequate?

198. What is the most common tool for helping define the detail?

199. Have you been able to easily identify success criteria and create objective measurements for each of the Cloud Database project scopes goal statements?

2.7 Assumption and Constraint Log: Cloud Database

200. Is there documentation of system capability requirements, data requirements, environment requirements, security requirements, and computer and hardware requirements?

201. Was the document/deliverable developed per the appropriate or required standards (for example, Institute of Electrical and Electronics Engineers standards)?

202. Is the current scope of the Cloud Database project substantially different than that originally defined in the approved Cloud Database project plan?

203. Is the steering committee active in Cloud Database project oversight?

204. When can log be discarded?

205. Are funding and staffing resource estimates sufficiently detailed and documented for use in planning and tracking the Cloud Database project?

206. Would known impacts serve as impediments?

207. Do documented requirements exist for all critical components and areas, including technical, business, interfaces, performance, security and conversion requirements?

208. How relevant is this attribute to this Cloud Database project or audit?

209. Is there a Steering Committee in place?

210. How are new requirements or changes to requirements identified?

211. Were the system requirements formally reviewed prior to initiating the design phase?

212. Does the plan conform to standards?

213. What worked well?

214. Are there ways to reduce the time it takes to get something approved?

215. Does the document/deliverable meet general requirements (for example, statement of work) for all deliverables?

216. Have Cloud Database project management standards and procedures been established and documented?

217. Should factors be unpredictable over time?

218. Does the document/deliverable meet all requirements (for example, statement of work) specific to this deliverable?

219. No superfluous information or marketing narrative?

2.8 Work Breakdown Structure: Cloud Database

220. Is it a change in scope?

221. When do you stop?

222. Where does it take place?

223. What is the probability that the Cloud Database project duration will exceed xx weeks?

224. How much detail?

225. How far down?

226. Why is it useful?

227. How big is a work-package?

228. What is the probability of completing the Cloud Database project in less that xx days?

229. What has to be done?

230. Can you make it?

231. When would you develop a Work Breakdown Structure?

232. Do you need another level?

233. Why would you develop a Work Breakdown

Structure?

234. How will you and your Cloud Database project team define the Cloud Database projects scope and work breakdown structure?

235. How many levels?

236. Who has to do it?

2.9 WBS Dictionary: Cloud Database

237. Are work packages reasonably short in time duration or do they have adequate objective indicators/milestones to minimize subjectivity of the in process work evaluation?

238. Are data elements summarized through the functional organizational structure for progressively higher levels of management?

239. Are significant decision points, constraints, and interfaces identified as key milestones?

240. Are the procedures for identifying indirect costs to incurring organizations, indirect cost pools, and allocating the costs from the pools to the contracts formally documented?

241. Budgets assigned to control accounts?

242. Cwbs elements to be subcontracted, with identification of subcontractors?

243. Is authorization of budgets in excess of the contract budget base controlled formally and done with the full knowledge and recognition of the procuring activity?

244. Does the contractors system include procedures for measuring the performance of critical subcontractors?

245. Contractor financial periods; for example,

annual?

246. Should you have a test for each code module?

247. Are data elements reconcilable between internal summary reports and reports forwarded to us?

248. Changes in the nature of the overhead requirements?

249. Are overhead budgets and costs being handled according to the disclosure statement when applicable, or otherwise properly classified (for example, engineering overhead, IR&D)?

250. What went right?

251. Intermediate schedules, as required, which provide a logical sequence from the master schedule to the control account level?

252. Does the contractor use objective results, design reviews and tests to trace schedule performance?

253. Budgets assigned to major functional organizations?

254. Are the requirements for all items of overhead established by rational, traceable processes?

2.10 Schedule Management Plan: Cloud Database

255. Was your organizations estimating methodology being used and followed?

256. Has a quality assurance plan been developed for the Cloud Database project?

257. Is there an excessive and invalid use of task constraints and relationships of leads/lags?

258. Is the schedule feasible and at what cost?

259. Has a structured approach been used to break work effort into manageable components (WBS)?

260. Identify the amount of schedule variation that triggers a warning. What happens if a warning is triggered?

261. Are schedule performance measures defined including pre-set triggers for specific actions?

262. Is there a formal set of procedures supporting Stakeholder Management?

263. Has a Cloud Database project Communications Plan been developed?

264. Have all documents been archived in a Cloud Database project repository for each release?

265. Have stakeholder accountabilities & responsibilities been clearly defined?

266. Are the Cloud Database project plans updated on a frequent basis?

267. Is there a formal process for updating the Cloud Database project baseline?

268. Is quality monitored from the perspective of the customers needs and expectations?

269. Has the ims content been baselined and is it adequately controlled?

270. Will rolling way planning be used?

271. Are the results of quality assurance reviews provided to affected groups & individuals?

272. Are staff skills known and available for each task?

2.11 Activity List: Cloud Database

273. What are the critical bottleneck activities?

274. How do you determine the late start (LS) for each activity?

275. What is the LF and LS for each activity?

276. How can the Cloud Database project be displayed graphically to better visualize the activities?

277. Can you determine the activity that must finish, before this activity can start?

278. Are the required resources available or need to be acquired?

279. Is there anything planned that does not need to be here?

280. For other activities, how much delay can be tolerated?

281. When will the work be performed?

282. How much slack is available in the Cloud Database project?

283. How should ongoing costs be monitored to try to keep the Cloud Database project within budget?

284. How detailed should a Cloud Database project get?

285. Who will perform the work?

286. What is your organizations history in doing similar activities?

287. What went wrong?

288. How will it be performed?

289. How difficult will it be to do specific activities on this Cloud Database project?

290. The wbs is developed as part of a joint planning session. and how do you know that youhave done this right?

291. What is the probability the Cloud Database project can be completed in xx weeks?

2.12 Activity Attributes: Cloud Database

292. Do you feel very comfortable with your prediction?

293. Is there a trend during the year?

294. What conclusions/generalizations can you draw from this?

295. Activity: fair or not fair?

296. Activity: what is In the Bag?

297. How many resources do you need to complete the work scope within a limit of X number of days?

298. Can more resources be added?

299. Would you consider either of corresponding activities an outlier?

300. Why?

301. How much activity detail is required?

302. What is missing?

303. How difficult will it be to complete specific activities on this Cloud Database project?

304. How do you manage time?

305. How else could the items be grouped?

306. Has management defined a definite timeframe for the turnaround or Cloud Database project window?

307. Time for overtime?

308. Resource is assigned to?

2.13 Milestone List: Cloud Database

309. Who will manage the Cloud Database project on a day-to-day basis?

310. Legislative effects?

311. Timescales, deadlines and pressures?

312. How soon can the activity finish?

313. Competitive advantages?

314. How late can each activity be finished and started?

315. How late can the activity start?

316. Identify critical paths (one or more) and which activities are on the critical path?

317. What is the market for your technology, product or service?

318. What date will the task finish?

319. Describe the concept of the technology, product or service that will be or has been developed. How will it be used?

320. Loss of key staff?

321. How late can the activity finish?

322. Level of the Innovation?

323. Continuity, supply chain robustness?

324. New USPs?

325. When will the Cloud Database project be complete?

326. Describe your organizations strengths and core competencies. What factors will make your organization succeed?

327. How will the milestone be verified?

2.14 Network Diagram: Cloud Database

328. What job or jobs follow it?

329. What activities must follow this activity?

330. What is the completion time?

331. What must be completed before an activity can be started?

332. If x is long, what would be the completion time if you break x into two parallel parts of y weeks and z weeks?

333. What job or jobs precede it?

334. How confident can you be in your milestone dates and the delivery date?

335. Where do you schedule uncertainty time?

336. What activities must occur simultaneously with this activity?

337. What are the tools?

338. Review the logical flow of the network diagram. Take a look at which activities you have first and then sequence the activities. Do they make sense?

339. What activity must be completed immediately

before this activity can start?

340. If a current contract exists, can you provide the vendor name, contract start, and contract expiration date?

341. Why must you schedule milestones, such as reviews, throughout the Cloud Database project?

342. What can be done concurrently?

343. What are the Key Success Factors?

344. Planning: who, how long, what to do?

345. What controls the start and finish of a job?

346. What job or jobs could run concurrently?

2.15 Activity Resource Requirements: Cloud Database

347. How many signatures do you require on a check and does this match what is in your policy and procedures?

348. Other support in specific areas?

349. Organizational Applicability?

350. Which logical relationship does the PDM use most often?

351. Anything else?

352. Why do you do that?

353. Do you use tools like decomposition and rolling-wave planning to produce the activity list and other outputs?

354. How do you handle petty cash?

355. What are constraints that you might find during the Human Resource Planning process?

356. What is the Work Plan Standard?

357. When does monitoring begin?

358. Are there unresolved issues that need to be addressed?

2.16 Resource Breakdown Structure: Cloud Database

359. What is each stakeholders desired outcome for the Cloud Database project?

360. What defines a successful Cloud Database project?

361. What defines a successful Cloud Database project?

362. Changes based on input from stakeholders?

363. How can this help you with team building?

364. Why is this important?

365. Who will use the system?

366. What is the difference between % Complete and % work?

367. How difficult will it be to do specific activities on this Cloud Database project?

368. When do they need the information?

369. Who will be used as a Cloud Database project team member?

370. What is the purpose of assigning and documenting responsibility?

371. Why do you do it?

372. Any changes from stakeholders?

373. Who is allowed to perform which functions?

374. What is the primary purpose of the human resource plan?

375. The list could probably go on, but, the thing that you would most like to know is, How long & How much?

2.17 Activity Duration Estimates: Cloud Database

376. Are contractor costs, schedule and technical performance monitored throughout the Cloud Database project?

377. Would you rate yourself as being risk-averse, risk-neutral, or risk-seeking?

378. Are actual Cloud Database project results compared with planned or expected results to determine the variance?

379. Does a process exist to identify individuals authorized to make certain decisions?

380. Is a contract developed which obligates the seller and the buyer?

381. What are the three main outputs of quality control?

382. Which suggestions do you find most useful?

383. Which would be the NEXT thing for the Cloud Database project manager to do?

384. Are operational definitions created to identify quality measurement criteria for specific activities?

385. If the optimiztic estimate for an activity is 12days, and the pessimistic estimate is 18days, what is the

standard deviation of this activity?

386. Are contingency plans created to prepare for risk events to occur?

387. Describe Cloud Database project integration management in your own words. How does Cloud Database project integration management relate to the Cloud Database project life cycle, stakeholders, and the other Cloud Database project management knowledge areas?

388. Are reward and recognition systems defined to promote or reinforce desired behavior?

389. Are updates on work results collected and used as inputs to the performance reporting process?

390. What tasks can take place concurrently?

391. How can software assist in Cloud Database project communications?

392. Who will promote it?

393. How does Cloud Database project integration management relate to the Cloud Database project life cycle, stakeholders, and the other Cloud Database project management knowledge areas?

2.18 Duration Estimating Worksheet: Cloud Database

394. Will the Cloud Database project collaborate with the local community and leverage resources?

395. Done before proceeding with this activity or what can be done concurrently?

396. What is your role?

397. Is this operation cost effective?

398. When does your organization expect to be able to complete it?

399. Define the work as completely as possible. What work will be included in the Cloud Database project?

400. What is the total time required to complete the Cloud Database project if no delays occur?

401. Do any colleagues have experience with your organization and/or RFPs?

402. What questions do you have?

403. Value pocket identification & quantification what are value pockets?

404. Science = process: remember the scientific method?

405. What is an Average Cloud Database project?

406. What work will be included in the Cloud Database project?

407. What is next?

408. Does the Cloud Database project provide innovative ways for stakeholders to overcome obstacles or deliver better outcomes?

409. Why estimate costs?

410. What utility impacts are there?

411. Small or large Cloud Database project?

2.19 Project Schedule: Cloud Database

412. Are there activities that came from a template or previous Cloud Database project that are not applicable on this phase of this Cloud Database project?

413. How can you fix it?

414. Cloud Database project work estimates Who is managing the work estimate quality of work tasks in the Cloud Database project schedule?

415. Your best shot for providing estimations how complex/how much work does the activity require?

416. What is the most mis-scheduled part of process?

417. Did the final product meet or exceed user expectations?

418. Was the Cloud Database project schedule reviewed by all stakeholders and formally accepted?

419. What is the purpose of a Cloud Database project schedule?

420. Why is this particularly bad?

421. What does that mean?

422. Are procedures defined by which the Cloud

Database project schedule may be changed?

423. Does the condition or event threaten the Cloud Database projects objectives in any ways?

424. How much slack is available in the Cloud Database project?

425. Are key risk mitigation strategies added to the Cloud Database project schedule?

426. Master Cloud Database project schedule?

427. Are quality inspections and review activities listed in the Cloud Database project schedule(s)?

428. Verify that the update is accurate. Are all remaining durations correct?

429. How does a Cloud Database project get to be a year late ?

2.20 Cost Management Plan: Cloud Database

430. Are issues raised, assessed, actioned, and resolved in a timely and efficient manner?

431. Similar Cloud Database projects?

432. Quality assurance overheads?

433. Has the business need been clearly defined?

434. Has a provision been made to reassess Cloud Database project risks at various Cloud Database project stages?

435. Weve met your goals?

436. Time management – how will the schedule impact of changes be estimated and approved?

437. Are tasks tracked by hours?

438. Is it possible to track all classes of Cloud Database project work (e.g. scheduled, un-scheduled, defect repair, etc.)?

439. Mitigation – based on the action, cost and probability of success, will the mitigation be made?

440. Are the Cloud Database project plans updated on a frequent basis?

441. Are the key elements of a Cloud Database project Charter present?

442. Is your organization certified as a supplier, wholesaler, regular dealer, or manufacturer of corresponding products/supplies?

443. Have process improvement efforts been completed before requirements efforts begin?

444. Are changes in deliverable commitments agreed to by all affected groups & individuals?

445. Will the forecasts be based on trend analysis and earned value statistics?

446. Are the schedule estimates reasonable given the Cloud Database project?

447. Have adequate resources been provided by management to ensure Cloud Database project success?

448. Have the key elements of a coherent Cloud Database project management strategy been established?

2.21 Activity Cost Estimates: Cloud Database

449. What cost data should be used to estimate costs during the 2-year follow-up period?

450. What do you want to know about the stay to know if costs were inappropriately high or low?

451. What is the activity inventory?

452. How many activities should you have?

453. What makes a good expected result statement?

454. Is costing method consistent with study goals?

455. Maintenance Reserve?

456. Does the activity serve a common type of customer?

457. What is the activity recast of the budget?

458. What are the audit requirements?

459. Were the tasks or work products prepared by the consultant useful?

460. Who determines the quality and expertise of contractors?

461. Are cost subtotals needed?

462. Was it performed on time?

463. What is a Cloud Database project Management Plan?

464. How Award?

465. Is there anything unique in this Cloud Database projects scope statement that will affect resources?

466. How do you change activities?

467. What is the Cloud Database projects sustainability strategy that will ensure Cloud Database project results will endure or be sustained?

2.22 Cost Estimating Worksheet: Cloud Database

468. Who is best positioned to know and assist in identifying corresponding factors?

469. What will others want?

470. Identify the timeframe necessary to monitor progress and collect data to determine how the selected measure has changed?

471. What info is needed?

472. Ask: are others positioned to know, are others credible, and will others cooperate?

473. How will the results be shared and to whom?

474. Does the Cloud Database project provide innovative ways for stakeholders to overcome obstacles or deliver better outcomes?

475. Can a trend be established from historical performance data on the selected measure and are the criteria for using trend analysis or forecasting methods met?

476. What can be included?

477. What happens to any remaining funds not used?

478. Will the Cloud Database project collaborate with

the local community and leverage resources?

479. What costs are to be estimated?

480. Is the Cloud Database project responsive to community need?

481. Is it feasible to establish a control group arrangement?

482. What additional Cloud Database project(s) could be initiated as a result of this Cloud Database project?

483. What is the estimated labor cost today based upon this information?

484. What is the purpose of estimating?

2.23 Cost Baseline: Cloud Database

485. What is it ?

486. Has the documentation relating to operation and maintenance of the product(s) or service(s) been delivered to, and accepted by, operations management?

487. Has the Cloud Database projected annual cost to operate and maintain the product(s) or service(s) been approved and funded?

488. What deliverables come first?

489. Have all approved changes to the schedule baseline been identified and impact on the Cloud Database project documented?

490. What does a good WBS NOT look like?

491. Have the lessons learned been filed with the Cloud Database project Management Office?

492. What threats might prevent you from getting there?

493. Does it impact schedule, cost, quality?

494. For what purpose ?

495. Is the requested change request a result of changes in other Cloud Database project(s)?

496. Are there contingencies or conditions related to the acceptance?

497. How do you manage cost?

498. Eac -estimate at completion, what is the total job expected to cost?

499. Does the suggested change request seem to represent a necessary enhancement to the product?

500. Have the resources used by the Cloud Database project been reassigned to other units or Cloud Database projects?

501. Who will use corresponding metrics ?

502. Will the Cloud Database project fail if the change request is not executed?

503. What is cost and Cloud Database project cost management?

504. How accurate do cost estimates need to be?

2.24 Quality Management Plan: Cloud Database

505. What has the QM Collaboration done?

506. How effectively was the Quality Management Plan applied during Cloud Database project Execution?

507. Why quality management?

508. How are changes approved?

509. Contradictory information between different documents?

510. Where do you focus?

511. How are people conducting sampling trained?

512. How do senior leaders create your organizational focus on customers and other stakeholders?

513. How does your organization address regulatory, legal, and ethical compliance?

514. Who else should be involved ?

515. How are deviations from procedures handled?

516. Would impacts defined serve as impediments?

517. When reporting to different audiences, do you

vary the form or type of report?

518. How are changes recorded?

519. Have you eliminated all duplicative tasks or manual efforts, where appropriate?

520. Results Available?

521. Who is responsible?

522. Who gets results of work?

523. How do senior leaders create an environment that encourages learning and innovation?

524. What data do you gather/use/compile?

2.25 Quality Metrics: Cloud Database

525. Is there a set of procedures to capture, analyze and act on quality metrics?

526. Was review conducted per standard protocols?

527. Why is now the time for quality metrics?

528. Were quality attributes reported?

529. How exactly do you define when differences exist?

530. Is the reporting frequency appropriate?

531. What level of statistical confidence do you use?

532. What if the biggest risk to your business were the already stated people who do not complain?

533. What forces exist that would cause them to change?

534. Where is quality now?

535. Did evaluation start on time?

536. How should customers provide input?

537. Are interface issues coordinated?

538. What are your organizations next steps?

539. Did the team meet the Cloud Database project success criteria documented in the Quality Metrics Matrix?

540. What metrics do you measure?

541. Do you stratify metrics by product or site?

542. Are quality metrics defined?

543. What do you measure?

544. Do you know how much profit a 10% decrease in waste would generate?

2.26 Process Improvement Plan: Cloud Database

545. What lessons have you learned so far?

546. If a process improvement framework is being used, which elements will help the problems and goals listed?

547. What is the test-cycle concept?

548. Has the time line required to move measurement results from the points of collection to databases or users been established?

549. Are you making progress on your improvement plan?

550. Are you making progress on the goals?

551. How do you manage quality?

552. Why do you want to achieve the goal?

553. Are you following the quality standards?

554. Has a process guide to collect the data been developed?

555. What actions are needed to address the problems and achieve the goals?

556. To elicit goal statements, do you ask a question

such as, What do you want to achieve?

557. Have the frequency of collection and the points in the process where measurements will be made been determined?

558. What makes people good SPI coaches?

559. Are you meeting the quality standards?

560. Are there forms and procedures to collect and record the data?

561. What personnel are the change agents for your initiative?

562. Modeling current processes is great, and will you ever see a return on that investment?

563. How do you measure?

2.27 Responsibility Assignment Matrix: Cloud Database

564. The already stated responsible for overhead performance control of related costs?

565. What are the deliverables?

566. Are work packages assigned to performing organizations?

567. Is work progressively subdivided into detailed work packages as requirements are defined?

568. What do people write/say on status/Cloud Database project reports?

569. Which resource planning tool provides information on resource responsibility and accountability?

570. Are data elements reconcilable between internal summary reports and reports forwarded to stakeholders?

571. Will too many Signing-off responsibilities delay the completion of the activity/deliverable?

572. Are people afraid to let you know when others are under allocated?

573. The staff characteristics – is the group or the person capable to work together as a team?

574. Not any rs, as, or cs: if an identified role is only informed, should others be eliminated from the matrix?

575. Budgeted cost for work performed?

576. How do you assist them to be as productive as possible?

577. Does the contractors system identify work accomplishment against the schedule plan?

578. How many hours by each staff member/rate?

2.28 Roles and Responsibilities: Cloud Database

579. What is working well within your organizations performance management system?

580. Do the values and practices inherent in the culture of your organization foster or hinder the process?

581. Are governance roles and responsibilities documented?

582. Once the responsibilities are defined for the Cloud Database project, have the deliverables, roles and responsibilities been clearly communicated to every participant?

583. Have you ever been a part of this team?

584. Was the expectation clearly communicated?

585. How is your work-life balance?

586. Are the quality assurance functions and related roles and responsibilities clearly defined?

587. What should you do now to ensure that you are meeting all expectations of your current position?

588. Does your vision/mission support a culture of quality data?

589. Concern: where are you limited or have no authority, where you can not influence?

590. Once the responsibilities are defined for the Cloud Database project, have the deliverables, roles and responsibilities been clearly communicated to every participant?

591. What should you do now to prepare for your career 5+ years from now?

592. Are your policies supportive of a culture of quality data?

593. Is the data complete?

594. What is working well?

595. Who is responsible for each task?

2.29 Human Resource Management Plan: Cloud Database

596. Is there an approved case?

597. Are the payment terms being followed?

598. What were things that you did very well and want to do the same again on the next Cloud Database project?

599. What skills, knowledge and experiences are required?

600. Is your organization heading towards expansion, outsourcing of certain talents or making cut-backs to save money?

601. Are Cloud Database project team roles and responsibilities identified and documented?

602. Have the key elements of a coherent Cloud Database project management strategy been established?

603. Is the manpower level sufficient to meet the future business requirements?

604. Does the resource management plan include a personnel development plan?

605. Are the right people being attracted and retained to meet the future challenges?

606. Does all Cloud Database project documentation reside in a common repository for easy access?

607. Has the scope management document been updated and distributed to help prevent scope creep?

608. Are vendor invoices audited for accuracy before payment?

609. Is it standard practice to formally commit stakeholders to the Cloud Database project via agreements?

610. Are schedule deliverables actually delivered?

611. Is a pmo (Cloud Database project management office) in place and provide oversight to the Cloud Database project?

612. Who are the people that make up your organization and whom create the success that your organization enjoys as a whole?

613. Are people being developed to meet the challenges of the future?

614. Is there an onboarding process in place?

2.30 Communications Management Plan: Cloud Database

615. What approaches do you use?

616. Which team member will work with each stakeholder?

617. Who did you turn to if you had questions?

618. Are others part of the communications management plan?

619. Are others needed?

620. What does the stakeholder need from the team?

621. Do you prepare stakeholder engagement plans?

622. Who to learn from?

623. Who will use or be affected by the result of a Cloud Database project?

624. How did the term stakeholder originate?

625. Do you have members of your team responsible for certain stakeholders?

626. Who were proponents/opponents?

627. In your work, how much time is spent on stakeholder identification?

628. Timing: when do the effects of the communication take place?

629. Are stakeholders internal or external?

630. Is the stakeholder role recognized by your organization?

631. What is Cloud Database project communications management?

632. Do you ask; can you recommend others for you to talk with about this initiative?

633. Which stakeholders are thought leaders, influences, or early adopters?

2.31 Risk Management Plan: Cloud Database

634. How is risk monitoring performed?

635. What things are likely to change?

636. Is this an issue, action item, question or a risk?

637. Is security a central objective?

638. Is the customer willing to establish rapid communication links with the developer?

639. What are the cost, schedule and resource impacts of avoiding the risk?

640. Litigation – what is the probability that lawsuits will cause problems or delays in the Cloud Database project?

641. How would you suggest monitoring for risk transition indicators?

642. Do you train all developers in the process?

643. Is the customer technically sophisticated in the product area?

644. How much risk protection can you afford?

645. Risk may be made during which step of risk management?

646. What does a risk management program do?

647. How can the process be made more effective or less cumbersome (process improvements)?

648. Risk probability and impact: how will the probabilities and impacts of risk items be assessed?

649. Mitigation -how can you avoid the risk?

650. How much risk can you tolerate?

651. Are tools for analysis and design available?

652. Financial risk -can your organization afford to undertake the Cloud Database project?

653. Where are you confronted with risks during the business phases?

2.32 Risk Register: Cloud Database

654. Schedule impact/severity estimated range (workdays) assume the event happens, what is the potential impact?

655. Is further information required before making a decision?

656. Are there other alternative controls that could be implemented?

657. Preventative actions - planned actions to reduce the likelihood a risk will occur and/or reduce the seriousness should it occur. What should you do now?

658. Market risk -will the new service or product be useful to your organization or marketable to others?

659. Do you require further engagement?

660. Which key risks have ineffective responses or outstanding improvement actions?

661. How is a Community Risk Register created?

662. Budget and schedule: what are the estimated costs and schedules for performing risk-related activities?

663. Have other controls and solutions been implemented in other services which could be applied as an alternative to additional funding?

664. Cost/benefit – how much will the proposed mitigations cost and how does this cost compare with the potential cost of the risk event/situation should it occur?

665. Assume the event happens, what is the Most Likely impact?

666. What would the impact to the Cloud Database project objectives be should the risk arise?

667. What are you going to do to limit the Cloud Database projects risk exposure due to the identified risks?

668. Methodology: how will risk management be performed on this Cloud Database project?

669. What may happen or not go according to plan?

670. Having taken action, how did the responses effect change, and where is the Cloud Database project now?

671. When is it going to be done?

672. What further options might be available for responding to the risk?

2.33 Probability and Impact Assessment: Cloud Database

673. Do you have a consistent repeatable process that is actually used?

674. Have decisions that should be left open because of inadequate information on technology been identified and responsibility assigned for reducing the uncertainty?

675. What is the experience (performance, attitude, business ethics, etc.) in the past with contractors?

676. How do risks change during the Cloud Database projects life cycle?

677. What risks does your organization have if the Cloud Database projects fail to meet deadline?

678. Will new information become available during the Cloud Database project?

679. What is the probability of the risk occurring?

680. Your customers business requirements have suddenly shifted because of a new regulatory statute, what now?

681. Do you manage the process through use of metrics?

682. What are the uncertainties associated with the

technology selected for the Cloud Database project?

683. Do requirements put excessive performance constraints on the product?

684. What are your data sources?

685. Who has experience with this?

686. What risks are necessary to achieve success?

687. What things might go wrong?

688. What will be the impact or consequence if the risk occurs?

689. What are the chances the event will occur?

690. Are formal technical reviews part of this process?

2.34 Probability and Impact Matrix: Cloud Database

691. Are people attending meetings and doing work?

692. What are the channels available for distribution to the customer?

693. What are the probable external agencies to act as Cloud Database project manager?

694. How well were you able to manage your risk?

695. Do you have specific methods that you use for each phase of the process?

696. Costs associated with late delivery or a defective product?

697. Are you working on the right risks?

698. Which is an input to the risk management process?

699. What will the damage be?

700. Prioritized components/features?

701. Which of your Cloud Database projects should be selected when compared with other Cloud Database projects?

702. Which phase of the Cloud Database project do

you take part in?

703. What is the likely future demand of the customer?

704. What action do you usually take against risks?

705. Economic to take on the Cloud Database project?

706. Do others match with the clients requirement?

707. Do requirements demand the use of new analysis, design, or testing methods?

708. What are the current demands of the customer?

2.35 Risk Data Sheet: Cloud Database

709. What if client refuses?

710. What are the main opportunities available to you that you should grab while you can?

711. What will be the consequences if it happens?

712. What can you do?

713. Whom do you serve (customers)?

714. Is the data sufficiently specified in terms of the type of failure being analyzed, and its frequency or probability?

715. What are you trying to achieve (Objectives)?

716. What is the likelihood of it happening?

717. Do effective diagnostic tests exist?

718. What is the chance that it will happen?

719. What was measured?

720. How can it happen?

721. What do people affected think about the need for, and practicality of preventive measures?

722. What are you weak at and therefore need to do better?

723. Has a sensitivity analysis been carried out?

724. How can hazards be reduced?

725. What do you know?

726. What are the main threats to your existence?

2.36 Procurement Management Plan: Cloud Database

727. Is there a Quality Management Plan?

728. Were escalated issues resolved promptly?

729. Is the communication plan being followed?

730. Have reserves been created to address risks?

731. Measurable - are the targets measurable?

732. Are Cloud Database project team members committed fulltime?

733. Has a Cloud Database project Communications Plan been developed?

734. Is there a procurement management plan in place?

735. Have external dependencies been captured in the schedule?

736. Are updated Cloud Database project time & resource estimates reasonable based on the current Cloud Database project stage?

737. Has the Cloud Database project manager been identified?

738. Are risk triggers captured?

739. Are Cloud Database project team members involved in detailed estimating and scheduling?

740. Has a quality assurance plan been developed for the Cloud Database project?

2.37 Source Selection Criteria: Cloud Database

741. How and when do you enter into Cloud Database project Procurement Management?

742. Do you want to have them collaborate at subfactor level?

743. How is past performance evaluated?

744. Do you ensure you evaluate what you asked for, not what you want to see or expect to see?

745. What procedures are followed when a contractor requires access to classified information or a significant quantity of special material/information?

746. What should be considered?

747. Who should attend debriefings?

748. What should be the contracting officers strategy?

749. Are types/quantities of material, facilities appropriate?

750. Does the evaluation of any change include an impact analysis; how will the change affect the scope, time, cost, and quality of the goods or services being provided?

751. What are the most critical evaluation criteria that

prove to be tiebreakers in the evaluation of proposals?

752. What instructions should be provided regarding oral presentations?

753. How should comments received in response to a RFP be handled?

754. Does your documentation identify why the team concurs or differs with reported performance from past performance report (CPARs, questionnaire responses, etc.)?

755. Are resultant proposal revisions allowed?

756. How do you manage procurement?

757. How can the methods of publicizing the buy be tailored to yield more effective price competition?

758. Do proposed hours support content and schedule?

759. Is a cost realism analysis used?

760. Are evaluators ready to begin this task?

2.38 Stakeholder Management Plan: Cloud Database

761. Has a Cloud Database project Communications Plan been developed?

762. Is stakeholder involvement adequate?

763. How many Cloud Database project staff does this specific process affect?

764. Are communication systems currently in place appropriate?

765. Do any protocols apply for records management?

766. Is there a formal set of procedures supporting Issues Management?

767. Will all relevant stakeholders be included within the review process?

768. Contradictory information between document sections?

769. Are corrective actions and variances reported?

770. Do Cloud Database project teams & team members report on status / activities / progress?

771. Are formal code reviews conducted?

772. Are the schedule estimates reasonable given the

Cloud Database project?

773. Is the performance of the supplier to be rated and documented?

774. What has to be purchased?

775. How accurate and complete is the information?

776. Has a sponsor been identified?

777. Are communication systems proposed compatible with staff skills and experience?

778. Are decisions captured in a decisions log?

2.39 Change Management Plan: Cloud Database

779. What work practices will be affected?

780. Where will the funds come from?

781. What are the dependencies?

782. Will all field readiness criteria have been practically met prior to training roll-out?

783. Has the training provider been established?

784. What does a resilient organization look like?

785. How badly can information be misinterpreted?

786. What prerequisite knowledge or training is required?

787. Are there any restrictions on who can receive the communications?

788. What communication network would you use – informal or formal?

789. What are the major changes to processes?

790. Has a training need analysis been carried out?

791. What are the needs, priorities and special interests of the audience?

792. Have the systems been configured and tested?

793. When does it make sense to customize?

794. What are the training strategies?

795. Has the priority for this Cloud Database project been set by the Business Unit Management Team?

796. Who might present the most resistance?

797. What skills, education, knowledge, or work experiences should the resources have for each identified competency?

3.0 Executing Process Group: Cloud Database

798. What are the critical steps involved in selecting measures and initiatives?

799. Do Cloud Database project managers understand your organizational context for Cloud Database projects?

800. What does it mean to take a systems view of a Cloud Database project?

801. What communication items need improvement?

802. What is involved in the solicitation process?

803. Why is it important to determine activity sequencing on Cloud Database projects?

804. In what way has the program come up with innovative measures for problem-solving?

805. If action is called for, what form should it take?

806. What Cloud Database projects and services are in the portfolio of your organization?

807. Who will provide training?

808. Is the Cloud Database project performing better or worse than planned?

809. How do you control progress of your Cloud Database project?

810. On which process should team members spend the most time?

811. What are crucial elements of successful Cloud Database project plan execution?

812. Will additional funds be needed for hardware or software?

813. What are the main types of goods and services being outsourced?

814. Will outside resources be needed to help?

815. Are decisions made in a timely manner?

816. How many different communication channels does the Cloud Database project team have?

3.1 Team Member Status Report: Cloud Database

817. How can you make it practical?

818. Why is it to be done?

819. Are your organizations Cloud Database projects more successful over time?

820. What is to be done?

821. The problem with Reward & Recognition Programs is that the truly deserving people all too often get left out. How can you make it practical?

822. Will the staff do training or is that done by a third party?

823. Are the products of your organizations Cloud Database projects meeting customers objectives?

824. How will resource planning be done?

825. When a teams productivity and success depend on collaboration and the efficient flow of information, what generally fails them?

826. How does this product, good, or service meet the needs of the Cloud Database project and your organization as a whole?

827. Does every department have to have a Cloud

Database project Manager on staff?

828. How much risk is involved?

829. Does your organization have the means (staff, money, contract, etc.) to produce or to acquire the product, good, or service?

830. Do you have an Enterprise Cloud Database project Management Office (EPMO)?

831. Does the product, good, or service already exist within your organization?

832. What specific interest groups do you have in place?

833. Are the attitudes of staff regarding Cloud Database project work improving?

834. How it is to be done?

835. Is there evidence that staff is taking a more professional approach toward management of your organizations Cloud Database projects?

3.2 Change Request: Cloud Database

836. Should staff call into the helpdesk or go to the website?

837. Have scm procedures for noting the change, recording it, and reporting it been followed?

838. Why do you want to have a change control system?

839. How many lines of code must be changed to implement the change?

840. How do team members communicate with each other?

841. Who has responsibility for approving and ranking changes?

842. What is the relationship between requirements attributes and attributes like complexity and size?

843. What is the change request log?

844. Has your address changed?

845. Does the schedule include Cloud Database project management time and change request analysis time?

846. Who can suggest changes?

847. Who is included in the change control team?

848. Are there requirements attributes that are strongly related to the occurrence of defects and failures?

849. How can changes be graded?

850. Are change requests logged and managed?

851. What are the Impacts to your organization?

852. Why control change across the life cycle?

853. Will all change requests be unconditionally tracked through this process?

854. What are the duties of the change control team?

855. Are there requirements attributes that are strongly related to the complexity and size?

3.3 Change Log: Cloud Database

856. How does this change affect scope?

857. Is the change request within Cloud Database project scope?

858. Is the change backward compatible without limitations?

859. Is the submitted change a new change or a modification of a previously approved change?

860. When was the request submitted?

861. Should a more thorough impact analysis be conducted?

862. Where do changes come from?

863. How does this change affect the timeline of the schedule?

864. Is the change request open, closed or pending?

865. Who initiated the change request?

866. Does the suggested change request represent a desired enhancement to the products functionality?

867. Is the requested change request a result of changes in other Cloud Database project(s)?

868. Will the Cloud Database project fail if the change

request is not executed?

869. Do the described changes impact on the integrity or security of the system?

870. Is this a mandatory replacement?

871. How does this relate to the standards developed for specific business processes?

872. When was the request approved?

3.4 Decision Log: Cloud Database

873. Behaviors; what are guidelines that the team has identified that will assist them with getting the most out of team meetings?

874. What makes you different or better than others companies selling the same thing?

875. What is the average size of your matters in an applicable measurement?

876. What alternatives/risks were considered?

877. What is your overall strategy for quality control / quality assurance procedures?

878. Linked to original objective?

879. How does provision of information, both in terms of content and presentation, influence acceptance of alternative strategies?

880. How does the use a Decision Support System influence the strategies/tactics or costs?

881. Meeting purpose; why does this team meet?

882. How effective is maintaining the log at facilitating organizational learning?

883. It becomes critical to track and periodically revisit both operational effectiveness; Are you noticing all that you need to, and are you interpreting what you

see effectively?

884. What eDiscovery problem or issue did your organization set out to fix or make better?

885. Do strategies and tactics aimed at less than full control reduce the costs of management or simply shift the cost burden?

886. With whom was the decision shared or considered?

887. How do you define success?

888. Who is the decisionmaker?

889. What are the cost implications?

890. Decision-making process; how will the team make decisions?

891. How do you know when you are achieving it?

892. Is everything working as expected?

3.5 Quality Audit: Cloud Database

893. How does your organization ensure that equipment is appropriately maintained and producing valid results?

894. How does the organization know that its industry and community engagement planning and management systems are appropriately effective and constructive in enabling relationships with key stakeholder groups?

895. Are all complaints involving the possible failure of a device, labeling, or packaging to meet any of its specifications reviewed, evaluated, and investigated?

896. How does your organization know that its system for commercializing research outputs is appropriately effective and constructive?

897. How do you indicate the extent to which your personnel would be expected to contribute to the work effort?

898. How does your organization know that its methods are appropriately effective and constructive?

899. Are goals well supported with strategies, operational plans, manuals and training?

900. How does your organization know that its relationships with the community at large are appropriately effective and constructive?

901. Are the policies and processes, as set out in the Quality Audit Manual, properly applied?

902. What has changed/improved as a result of the review processes?

903. What data about organizational performance is routinely collected and reported?

904. What review processes are in place for your organizations major activities?

905. What experience do staff have in the type of work that the audit entails?

906. How does your organization know that its teaching activities (and staff learning) are effectively and constructively enhanced by its activities?

907. How does your organization know that it is maintaining a conducive staff climate?

908. Are people allowed to contribute ideas?

909. Are the review comments incorporated?

910. Is refuse and garbage adequately stored and disposed of with sufficient frequency to prevent contamination?

911. How well do you think your organization engages with the outside community?

912. Have personnel cleanliness and health requirements been established?

3.6 Team Directory: Cloud Database

913. Is construction on schedule?

914. Contract requirements complied with?

915. Who are the Team Members?

916. Who will be the stakeholders on your next Cloud Database project?

917. Where should the information be distributed?

918. When does information need to be distributed?

919. Process decisions: do invoice amounts match accepted work in place?

920. How will the team handle changes?

921. Process decisions: do job conditions warrant additional actions to collect job information and document on-site activity?

922. Days from the time the issue is identified?

923. Who will report Cloud Database project status to all stakeholders?

924. Where will the product be used and/or delivered or built when appropriate?

925. Why is the work necessary?

926. Process decisions: are contractors adequately prosecuting the work?

927. Have you decided when to celebrate the Cloud Database projects completion date?

928. Process decisions: is work progressing on schedule and per contract requirements?

929. Process decisions: are all start-up, turn over and close out requirements of the contract satisfied?

930. Who will write the meeting minutes and distribute?

931. How will you accomplish and manage the objectives?

932. Decisions: what could be done better to improve the quality of the constructed product?

3.7 Team Operating Agreement: Cloud Database

933. Have you set the goals and objectives of the team?

934. What is teaming?

935. What types of accommodations will be formulated and put in place for sustaining the team?

936. Confidentiality: how will confidential information be handled?

937. Are there influences outside the team that may affect performance, and if so, have you identified and addressed them?

938. Do you use a parking lot for any items that are important and outside of the agenda?

939. Did you delegate tasks such as taking meeting minutes, presenting a topic and soliciting input?

940. Do you upload presentation materials in advance and test the technology?

941. Are there more than two functional areas represented by your team?

942. Do you post meeting notes and the recording (if used) and notify participants?

943. Do you solicit member feedback about meetings and what would make them better?

944. Do you prevent individuals from dominating the meeting?

945. Resource allocation: how will individual team members account for time and expenses, and how will this be allocated in the team budget?

946. Methodologies: how will key team processes be implemented, such as training, research, work deliverable production, review and approval processes, knowledge management, and meeting procedures?

947. Do you record meetings for the already stated unable to attend?

948. Do you determine the meeting length and time of day?

949. Did you determine the technology methods that best match the messages to be communicated?

950. Is compensation based on team and individual performance?

951. Do you vary your voice pace, tone and pitch to engage participants and gain involvement?

952. Has the appropriate access to relevant data and analysis capability been granted?

3.8 Team Performance Assessment: Cloud Database

953. To what degree does the team possess adequate membership to achieve its ends?

954. To what degree are the skill areas critical to team performance present?

955. When a reviewer complains about method variance, what is the essence of the complaint?

956. If you have criticized someones work for method variance in your role as reviewer, what was the circumstance?

957. To what degree does the teams work approach provide opportunity for members to engage in results-based evaluation?

958. Do friends perform better than acquaintances?

959. Does more radicalness mean more perceived benefits?

960. To what degree are fresh input and perspectives systematically caught and added (for example, through information and analysis, new members, and senior sponsors)?

961. To what degree does the teams work approach provide opportunity for members to engage in open interaction?

962. To what degree can team members meet frequently enough to accomplish the teams ends?

963. To what degree do the goals specify concrete team work products?

964. Do you promptly inform members about major developments that may affect them?

965. How do you manage human resources?

966. How do you encourage members to learn from each other?

967. To what degree do members understand and articulate the same purpose without relying on ambiguous abstractions?

968. To what degree are the members clear on what they are individually responsible for and what they are jointly responsible for?

969. Is there a particular method of data analysis that you would recommend as a means of demonstrating that method variance is not of great concern for a given dataset?

970. To what degree can the team ensure that all members are individually and jointly accountable for the teams purpose, goals, approach, and work-products?

971. To what degree are staff involved as partners in the improvement process?

972. To what degree do team members articulate the teams work approach?

3.9 Team Member Performance Assessment: Cloud Database

973. What evaluation results did you have?

974. What is a significant fact or event?

975. Who they are?

976. How are assessments designed, delivered, and otherwise used to maximize training?

977. How will you identify your Team Leaders?

978. How do you currently use the time that is available?

979. What are best practices for delivering and developing training evaluations to maximize the benefits of leveraging emerging technologies?

980. What steps have you taken to improve performance?

981. What is collaboration?

982. How often are assessments to be conducted?

983. How do you implement Cost Reduction?

984. Does platform-specific assessment information contribute to training placement or tailoring of instruction (e.g. aptitude-treatment interaction)?

985. Goals met?

986. What are the evaluation strategies (e.g., reaction, learning, behavior, results) used. What evaluation results did you have?

987. How accurately is your plan implemented?

988. What happens if a team member disagrees with the Job Expectations?

989. Does the rater (supervisor) have to wait for the interim or final performance assessment review to tell an employee that the employees performance is unsatisfactory?

990. What evidence supports your decision-making?

991. Does statute or regulation require the job responsibility?

3.10 Issue Log: Cloud Database

992. Who is the issue assigned to?

993. Is the issue log kept in a safe place?

994. Why multiple evaluators?

995. How much time does it take to do it?

996. Who reported the issue?

997. Who is involved as you identify stakeholders?

998. Do you feel more overwhelmed by stakeholders?

999. Are the stakeholders getting the information they need, are they consulted, are concerns addressed?

1000. Do you feel a register helps?

1001. Is access to the Issue Log controlled?

1002. Are stakeholder roles recognized by your organization?

1003. Are they needed?

1004. Can you think of other people who might have concerns or interests?

1005. Who do you turn to if you have questions?

1006. What would have to change?

1007. Who have you worked with in past, similar initiatives?

4.0 Monitoring and Controlling Process Group: Cloud Database

1008. How well defined and documented were the Cloud Database project management processes you chose to use?

1009. How should needs be met?

1010. Have operating capacities been created and/or reinforced in partners?

1011. Where is the Risk in the Cloud Database project?

1012. Is the schedule for the set products being met?

1013. Feasibility: how much money, time, and effort can you put into this?

1014. If a risk event occurs, what will you do?

1015. Does the solution fit in with organizations technical architectural requirements?

1016. Is there undesirable impact on staff or resources?

1017. What resources are necessary?

1018. Is it what was agreed upon?

1019. Where is the Risk in the Cloud Database project?

1020. Is there sufficient funding available for this?

1021. Were decisions made in a timely manner?

1022. User: who wants the information and what are they interested in?

1023. Accuracy: what design will lead to accurate information?

1024. Use: how will they use the information?

4.1 Project Performance Report: Cloud Database

1025. What is the degree to which rules govern information exchange between groups?

1026. To what degree do team members understand one anothers roles and skills?

1027. To what degree are the structures of the formal organization consistent with the behaviors in the informal organization?

1028. To what degree do team members frequently explore the teams purpose and its implications?

1029. To what degree are the teams goals and objectives clear, simple, and measurable?

1030. To what degree does the formal organization make use of individual resources and meet individual needs?

1031. To what degree is there centralized control of information sharing?

1032. To what degree is there a sense that only the team can succeed?

1033. To what degree can team members frequently and easily communicate with one another?

1034. To what degree can the cognitive capacity of

individuals accommodate the flow of information?

1035. What is the PRS?

1036. To what degree does the task meet individual needs?

1037. How can Cloud Database project sustainability be maintained?

1038. To what degree does the information network communicate information relevant to the task?

1039. How will procurement be coordinated with other Cloud Database project aspects, such as scheduling and performance reporting?

1040. To what degree do members articulate the goals beyond the team membership?

1041. What degree are the relative importance and priority of the goals clear to all team members?

1042. To what degree does the information network provide individuals with the information they require?

1043. To what degree do all members feel responsible for all agreed-upon measures?

4.2 Variance Analysis: Cloud Database

1044. How are material, labor, and overhead variances calculated and recorded?

1045. Are the bases and rates for allocating costs from each indirect pool consistently applied?

1046. What business event causes fluctuations?

1047. Are material costs reported within the same period as that in which BCWP is earned for that material?

1048. Can the relationship with problem customers be restructured so that there is a win-win situation?

1049. Did your organization lose existing customers and/or gain new customers?

1050. Can the contractor substantiate work package and planning package budgets?

1051. Are detailed work packages planned as far in advance as practicable?

1052. Are your organizations and items of cost assigned to each pool identified?

1053. Is the market likely to continue to grow at this rate next year?

1054. Other relevant issues of Variance Analysis -selling price or gross margin?

1055. Are overhead costs budgets established on a basis consistent with the anticipated direct business base?

1056. Are there knowledgeable Cloud Database projections of future performance?

1057. The anticipated business volume?

1058. How does the monthly budget compare to the actual experience?

1059. How does your organization measure performance?

1060. What is the budgeted cost for work scheduled?

1061. Are the actual costs used for variance analysis reconcilable with data from the accounting system?

1062. How are variances affected by multiple material and labor categories?

1063. Are the wbs and organizational levels for application of the Cloud Database projected overhead costs identified?

4.3 Earned Value Status: Cloud Database

1064. Where are your problem areas?

1065. If earned value management (EVM) is so good in determining the true status of a Cloud Database project and Cloud Database project its completion, why is it that hardly any one uses it in information systems related Cloud Database projects?

1066. How much is it going to cost by the finish?

1067. How does this compare with other Cloud Database projects?

1068. Where is evidence-based earned value in your organization reported?

1069. Verification is a process of ensuring that the developed system satisfies the stakeholders agreements and specifications; Are you building the product right? What do you verify?

1070. When is it going to finish?

1071. Earned value can be used in almost any Cloud Database project situation and in almost any Cloud Database project environment. it may be used on large Cloud Database projects, medium sized Cloud Database projects, tiny Cloud Database projects (in cut-down form), complex and simple Cloud Database projects and in any market sector. some people, of course, know all about earned value, they have used it for years - but perhaps not as effectively as they could have?

1072. Validation is a process of ensuring that the developed system will actually achieve the stakeholders desired outcomes; Are you building the right product? What do you validate?

1073. Are you hitting your Cloud Database projects targets?

1074. What is the unit of forecast value?

4.4 Risk Audit: Cloud Database

1075. Are you meeting your legal, regulatory and compliance requirements - if not, why not?

1076. What impact does experience with one client have on decisions made for other clients during the risk-assessment process?

1077. Are some people working on multiple Cloud Database projects?

1078. Whence the business risk audit?

1079. Who is responsible for what?

1080. Is the customer willing to participate in reviews?

1081. What events or circumstances could affect the achievement of your objectives?

1082. How are risk appetites expressed?

1083. Have risks been considered with an insurance broker or provider and suitable insurance cover been arranged?

1084. Does your organization have an up-to-date constitution?

1085. Estimated size of product in number of programs, files, transactions?

1086. Are team members trained in the use of the

tools?

1087. What are the strategic implications with clients when auditors focus audit resources based on business-level risks?

1088. What is the effect of globalisation; is business becoming too complex and can the auditor rely on auditing standards?

1089. How risk averse are you?

1090. Who audits the auditor?

1091. What expertise does the Board have on quality, outcomes, and errors?

1092. Has risk management been considered when planning an event?

1093. Do you have financial policies and procedures in place to guide officers of your organization/treasurer/general members?

1094. Are Cloud Database project requirements stable?

4.5 Contractor Status Report: Cloud Database

1095. How long have you been using the services?

1096. What are the minimum and optimal bandwidth requirements for the proposed solution?

1097. Who can list a Cloud Database project as organization experience, your organization or a previous employee of your organization?

1098. How is risk transferred?

1099. What was the actual budget or estimated cost for your organizations services?

1100. What was the final actual cost?

1101. How does the proposed individual meet each requirement?

1102. Describe how often regular updates are made to the proposed solution. Are corresponding regular updates included in the standard maintenance plan?

1103. What process manages the contracts?

1104. What was the overall budget or estimated cost?

1105. Are there contractual transfer concerns?

1106. What is the average response time for

answering a support call?

1107. What was the budget or estimated cost for your organizations services?

1108. If applicable; describe your standard schedule for new software version releases. Are new software version releases included in the standard maintenance plan?

4.6 Formal Acceptance: Cloud Database

1109. Do you perform formal acceptance or burn-in tests?

1110. Does it do what client said it would?

1111. Was the Cloud Database project managed well?

1112. Who would use it?

1113. Was the Cloud Database project work done on time, within budget, and according to specification?

1114. Was business value realized?

1115. How does your team plan to obtain formal acceptance on your Cloud Database project?

1116. Was the sponsor/customer satisfied?

1117. Did the Cloud Database project manager and team act in a professional and ethical manner?

1118. Do you buy pre-configured systems or build your own configuration?

1119. What function(s) does it fill or meet?

1120. Who supplies data?

1121. What can you do better next time?

1122. Does it do what Cloud Database project team said it would?

1123. Do you buy-in installation services?

1124. Was the Cloud Database project goal achieved?

1125. How well did the team follow the methodology?

1126. Have all comments been addressed?

1127. What features, practices, and processes proved to be strengths or weaknesses?

1128. What was done right?

5.0 Closing Process Group: Cloud Database

1129. What is the overall risk of the Cloud Database project to your organization?

1130. Did the Cloud Database project team have the right skills?

1131. Is this a follow-on to a previous Cloud Database project?

1132. Is this an updated Cloud Database project Proposal Document?

1133. What level of risk does the proposed budget represent to the Cloud Database project?

1134. What is the risk of failure to your organization?

1135. How will you know you did it?

1136. Was the user/client satisfied with the end product?

1137. Were the outcomes different from the already stated planned?

1138. What areas were overlooked on this Cloud Database project?

1139. How dependent is the Cloud Database project on other Cloud Database projects or work efforts?

1140. Is the Cloud Database project funded?

1141. Were sponsors and decision makers available when needed outside regularly scheduled meetings?

1142. How well did the chosen processes fit the needs of the Cloud Database project?

1143. Were risks identified and mitigated?

1144. Did the delivered product meet the specified requirements and goals of the Cloud Database project?

1145. Were cost budgets met?

1146. What were things that you need to improve?

5.1 Procurement Audit: Cloud Database

1147. Are payment generated from computer programs reviewed by supervisory personnel prior to distribution?

1148. If an electronic auction or a dynamic purchasing system was used, did the tender documents specify details on access to information, electronic equipment used and connection specifications?

1149. Were additional works charged at the unit prices agreed in the initial contract?

1150. Did your organization state the minimum requirements to be met by the variants in the tender documents?

1151. When performance conditions were detailed in the tender documentation, did the contracting authority verify if the tenders received met the already stated requirements?

1152. Does your organization have an overall strategy and/or policy on public procurement, providing guidance for procuring entities?

1153. Were the specifications of the contract determined free from influence of particular interests of consultants, experts or other economic operators?

1154. Are risks in the external environment identified,

for example: Budgetary constraints?

1155. In case of decisions not to conclude a procurement or award a contract, were tenderers informed in writing and on a timely basis of the already stated decisions and grounds?

1156. Do procedures require cash advances to be returned by transferred or terminated employees before they can receive final paychecks?

1157. Does the strategy contain incentives to evaluate the performance of the procurement function/unit?

1158. Are controls proportionated to risks?

1159. Are incentives to deliver on time and in quantity properly specified?

1160. Are all purchase orders reviewed by someone other than the individual preparing the purchase order (reasonableness of order and vendor selection)?

1161. Was the admissibility of variants displayed in the contract notice?

1162. Where applicable, did your organization adequately manage experts employed to assist in the procurement process?

1163. Where required, were candidates registered as approved contractors, suppliers or service providers or certified by relevant bodies?

1164. Has an upper limit of cost been fixed?

1165. Were any additional works or deliveries admissible, without recourse to a new procurement procedure?

1166. Are there mechanisms in place to evaluate the performance of the departments suppliers?

5.2 Contract Close-Out: Cloud Database

1167. Change in circumstances?

1168. How is the contracting office notified of the automatic contract close-out?

1169. What happens to the recipient of services?

1170. Was the contract complete without requiring numerous changes and revisions?

1171. Change in knowledge?

1172. Are the signers the authorized officials?

1173. Have all contract records been included in the Cloud Database project archives?

1174. Was the contract type appropriate?

1175. Was the contract sufficiently clear so as not to result in numerous disputes and misunderstandings?

1176. Parties: Authorized?

1177. What is capture management?

1178. Have all contracts been closed?

1179. Has each contract been audited to verify acceptance and delivery?

1180. Have all contracts been completed?

1181. Have all acceptance criteria been met prior to final payment to contractors?

1182. How/when used ?

1183. Change in attitude or behavior?

1184. Parties: who is involved?

1185. How does it work?

5.3 Project or Phase Close-Out: Cloud Database

1186. What were the actual outcomes?

1187. What hierarchical authority does the stakeholder have in your organization?

1188. What went well?

1189. Who are the Cloud Database project stakeholders and what are roles and involvement?

1190. What are the marketing communication needs for each stakeholder?

1191. Is the lesson based on actual Cloud Database project experience rather than on independent research?

1192. Did the delivered product meet the specified requirements and goals of the Cloud Database project?

1193. What can you do better next time, and what specific actions can you take to improve?

1194. Can the lesson learned be replicated?

1195. Were messages directly related to the release strategy or phases of the Cloud Database project?

1196. Is there a clear cause and effect between the

activity and the lesson learned?

1197. What could have been improved?

1198. Is the lesson significant, valid, and applicable?

1199. What is this stakeholder expecting?

1200. Planned remaining costs?

1201. Complete yes or no?

1202. Planned completion date?

1203. In addition to assessing whether the Cloud Database project was successful, it is equally critical to analyze why it was or was not fully successful. Are you including this?

1204. Who is responsible for award close-out?

1205. In preparing the Lessons Learned report, should it reflect a consensus viewpoint, or should the report reflect the different individual viewpoints?

5.4 Lessons Learned: Cloud Database

1206. How effective was the architecture/system design process?

1207. How well were expectations met regarding the frequency and content of information that was conveyed to by the Cloud Database project Manager?

1208. How useful was the format and content of the Cloud Database project Status Report to you?

1209. Will the information remain current?

1210. Why does your organization need a lessons learned (LL) capability?

1211. What is the proportion of in-house and contractor personnel authorized for the Cloud Database project?

1212. What did you put in place to ensure success?

1213. How effectively and timely was your organizational change impact identified and planned for?

1214. Did the delivered product meet the specified requirements and goals of the Cloud Database project?

1215. What are the influence patterns?

1216. What were the main bottlenecks on the

process?

1217. What are the performance measures?

1218. What specialization does the task require?

1219. What is in the future?

1220. How useful do individuals find communications?

1221. How well did the Cloud Database project Manager respond to questions or comments related to the Cloud Database project?

1222. How effectively were issues managed on the Cloud Database project?

1223. How well is the build process working?

1224. What solutions or recommendations can you offer that would have improved some aspect of the Cloud Database project?

Index

commitment   95, 119
committed   67, 204
Committee   147-148
common   146, 174, 191
community   138, 168, 177, 196, 222-223
companies   1, 97, 220
company   7, 43, 63, 103-104, 115-117, 123
compare   63, 84, 197, 240-241
compared   102, 166, 200
comparing   79
comparison   10
compatible   209, 218
compelling   28
competency   211
competing   45
compile   181
complain   182
complains   228
complaint   228
complaints   222
complete   1, 8, 10, 20, 31, 39, 157, 160, 164, 168, 189, 209,
254, 257
completed   11, 28, 39, 127, 156, 161, 173, 255
completely   106, 168
completing   123, 149
completion   32, 161, 179, 186, 225, 241, 257
complex   7, 117, 134, 170, 241, 244
complexity   21, 53, 216-217
compliance   20, 48, 69, 80, 180, 243
complied   224
components   137, 147, 153, 200
comprise   132
compute   11
computer   147, 251
computing   106
concept   73, 159, 184
concern   52, 80, 189, 229
concerned   16
concerns   16, 22, 109, 233, 245
conclude   252
concrete   78, 229
concurs   207
condition   94, 171

267

mantle 120
Manual   181, 223
manuals   222
Mapping   59, 61, 64
margin 239
market 19, 159, 196, 239, 241
marketable   196
marketer   7
marketing   103, 148, 256
markets   24
Master 152, 171
material   127, 206, 239-240
materials   1, 226
matrices   143
Matrix 2-4, 130, 143, 183, 186-187, 200
matter 29, 48, 50
matters   220
mature 138
maximize   231
maximizing   122
maximum   125
meaningful   53, 112
measurable   31, 38, 204, 237
measure   2, 9, 15, 17, 29, 39, 41-42, 46-51, 53, 63, 69, 71, 73,
78-79, 82, 90-91, 93-94, 132, 176, 183, 185, 240
measured   24, 42-43, 47-48, 50-51, 78, 87, 96, 202
measures   45, 48-49, 51, 53, 58, 60, 63, 66, 80, 92, 94, 98,
133, 153, 202, 212, 238, 259
measuring   90, 151
mechanical   1
mechanisms   136, 253
medium   241
meeting   34, 36, 91, 136, 185, 188, 214, 220, 225-227, 243
meetings   32, 36, 136, 145, 200, 220, 227, 250
megatrends   106
member   5, 35, 119, 164, 187, 192, 214, 227, 231-232
members   36, 92, 136, 139, 145, 192, 204-205, 208, 213, 216,
224, 227-230, 237-238, 243-244
membership   228, 238
Mentally   139
message   90
messages   227, 256
method   48, 132, 168, 174, 228-229

particular   58, 229, 251
Parties 80, 254-255
partners   20, 32, 80, 95, 111, 117, 121, 133, 229, 235
patterns   81, 258
paycheck   103
paychecks   252
paying 117
payment   190-191, 251, 255
pending   218
people 7, 18, 51, 64, 82, 88, 93, 100, 102-103, 107-110, 113, 116,
118, 121, 180, 182, 185-186, 190-191, 200, 202, 214, 223, 233, 241,
243
perceive   105
perceived   228
percentage   143
perception   75, 79, 103
perform   18, 35-36, 134, 138, 156, 165, 228, 247
performed   73, 143, 155-156, 175, 187, 194, 197
performing   186, 196, 212
perhaps   19, 242
period 76, 174, 239
periods 151
permission   1
person 1, 24, 130, 186
personal   121
personally   143
personnel   16, 68, 88, 137, 185, 190, 222-223, 251, 258
pertinent   88
phases 42, 132, 139, 195, 256
phrase 139
pitfalls 101
placement   231
planet 88
planned   88, 96-97, 126, 139, 155, 166, 196, 212, 239, 249,
257-258
planners   94
planning   3, 8, 92, 125, 128, 132, 147, 154, 156, 162-163,
186, 214, 222, 239, 244
pocket 168
pockets   168
points 25, 39, 54, 70, 85, 98, 123, 151, 184-185
policies   189, 223, 244
policy 34, 83, 94, 132, 163, 251

problem   15-19, 21, 23, 26, 29-30, 38, 43, 49, 57, 63, 142, 214, 221, 239, 241

problems   16-19, 22, 25, 76, 83-84, 93, 122, 141, 184, 194

procedure   253

procedures   9, 58, 77, 91, 98, 136, 148, 151, 153, 163, 170, 180, 182, 185, 206, 208, 216, 220, 227, 244, 252

proceeding   168

process   1-7, 9, 28-29, 38-39, 47, 55-65, 67-69, 74-75, 87, 89-95, 125, 127, 132-133, 137, 139, 141-143, 145, 151, 154, 163, 166-168, 170, 173, 184-185, 188, 191, 194-195, 198-200, 208, 212-213, 217, 221, 224-225, 229, 235, 241-243, 245, 249, 252, 258-259

processes   43, 48, 57-60, 62-63, 65-67, 88, 90-91, 125, 130-131, 136, 152, 185, 210, 219, 223, 227, 235, 248, 250

procuring   151, 251

produce   55, 125, 163, 215

produced   72

producing   143, 222

product   1, 53, 60, 63, 113-114, 138, 140, 146, 159, 170, 178-179, 183, 194, 196, 199-200, 214-215, 224-225, 241-243, 249-250, 256, 258

production   39, 73, 107, 227

productive   187

products   1, 19, 21, 51, 104, 120, 127, 133, 143, 173-174, 214, 218, 229, 235

profit   183

program   20, 46, 66, 94, 132-133, 195, 212

programs   214, 243, 251

progress   38, 47, 73, 89, 111, 133, 176, 184, 208, 213

project 2-8, 18, 20, 23, 39, 52, 62, 66-67, 84, 88, 96-97, 104, 108-110, 112, 115, 117-119, 124-134, 136-139, 141, 143, 145-150, 153-160, 162, 164, 166-173, 175-180, 183, 186, 188-195, 197-201, 204-206, 208-209, 211-216, 218, 224, 235, 237-238, 241, 244-245, 247-250, 254, 256-259

projected   178, 240

projects   2, 52, 117, 124, 127, 131, 133, 136, 143, 150, 171-172, 175, 179, 197-198, 200, 212, 214-215, 225, 241-243, 249

promising   113

promote   51, 167

promptly   204, 229

proofing   74

proper 97

properly   37, 152, 223, 252

proponents   192

starting9
start-up   225
stated 120, 182, 186, 227, 249, 251-252
statement   3, 10, 83-84, 137, 139, 145, 148, 152, 174-175
statements   11, 25, 38, 40, 54, 57, 70, 85, 98, 123, 146, 184
statistics   173
Status 5-6, 136, 186, 208, 214, 224, 241, 245, 258
statute 198, 232
steady 46
Steering   147-148
stored 223
stories 29
strategic   42, 74, 89, 115, 244
strategies   96, 101, 115, 145, 171, 211, 220-222, 232
strategy   17, 33, 45, 72, 75, 79, 98, 102, 105, 109, 122, 173,
175, 190, 206, 220, 251-252, 256
stratify 183
Stream 59, 64
strengths   160, 248
stretch 118
strict   62
strive   118
Strongly   10, 15, 26, 41, 55, 71, 87, 100, 217
structure   3, 47, 84, 114, 117, 146, 149-151, 164
structured   103, 153
structures   237
stubborn   107
stupid 106
subdivided   186
subfactor   206
subject8-9, 29
submitted   218
subset 23
subtotals   174
succeed   43, 117, 160, 237
success   17, 24, 32-33, 36, 39, 41, 43, 46, 50, 74, 79, 82-83,
96, 106, 108-110, 113, 122, 126-127, 133, 146, 162, 172-173, 183,
191, 199, 214, 221, 258
successes   102
successful   63, 85, 97, 101, 108-109, 127, 132, 164, 213-214,
257
succession   97
suddenly   198